The
AUSTERITY
BOOK

The
AUSTERITY
BOOK

Classic tips for enjoying life inexpensively

Compiled by

JAQUELINE MITCHELL

OSPREY
PUBLISHING

First published in Great Britain in 2011 by Osprey Publishing,
Midland House, West Way, Botley, Oxford, OX2 0PH, UK
44-02 23rd Street, Suite 219, Long Island City, NY 11101, USA
E-mail: info@ospreypublishing.com

Introduction, selection and compilation © 2011 Jaqueline Mitchell

Published in America and Canada as *The Good Life On a Budget*.

NOTE:

Readers should note that while all materials in this book have been faithfully reprinted
as in the original texts, the instructions given are not intended to replace manufacturers'
guidance regarding use of tools, chemicals, ingredients and other materials. Always
follow the safety guidelines. The contents of this book were originally produced in
another time and in another context, and readers should take the usual precautions in
handling materials and tools and in preparation of recipes and so on. People with special
dietary or other requirements of any kind should consult appropriate professionals
before proceeding. The compiler and publisher disclaim any liability for loss, injury or
damage incurred as a consequence, directly or indirectly, of the use and application of
the contents of this book.

Every attempt has been made by the Publisher to secure the appropriate permissions for material
reproduced in this book. If there has been any oversight we will be happy to rectify the situation
and written submission should be made to the Publishers.

A CIP catalogue record for this book is available from the British Library

ISBN: 978 1 84908 530 4

Cover design and page layout by Myriam Bell Design, France
Typeset in Cochin and Birch
Originated by PDQ Media, Bungay, UK
Printed in China through Worldprint Ltd

11 12 13 14 15   10 9 8 7 6 5 4 3 2 1

Imperial War Museum Collections

Many of the photos in this book come from the Imperial War Museum's huge collections
which cover all aspects of conflict involving Britain and the Commonwealth since the start of
the twentieth century. These rich resources are available online to search, browse and buy at
www.iwmcollections.org.uk. In addition to Collections Online, you can visit the Visitor Rooms
where you can explore over 8 million photographs, thousands of hours of moving images, the
largest sound archive of its kind in the world, thousands of diaries and letters written by people
in wartime, and a huge reference library. To make an appointment, call (020) 7416 5320.

Imperial War Museum
www.iwm.org.uk

Osprey Publishing is supporting the Woodland Trust, the UK's leading woodland conservation
charity, by funding the dedication of trees.

www.ospreypublishing.com

CONTENTS

INTRODUCTION

In 1945, when the cook and writer Elizabeth David returned from shopping in Kensington, London, and took fresh tomatoes out of her basket, her sister was moved to tears. 'It's just that I've been trying to buy fresh tomatoes for five years' she said. At the war's end, people expected things to become easier, but in fact they became worse. 'Where was the transformation?' wondered Susan Cooper looking back on the period, 'We still bathed in water that wouldn't come over your knees unless you flattened them; we still wore clothes with the ugly "Utility" half-moons on the label.' America's Lend-Lease programme was terminated and six years of war left Britain in the economic doldrums. Hugh Dalton's 1947 Austerity Budget was an indication of what was to come; by 1948 rations were lower than they had been during the war. America also experienced rationing, while the post-war situation in Europe was far worse. There were hard times ahead.

The period between the end of the Second World War and the end of rationing in 1954 was one of austerity. Rationing in Britain had been introduced in 1940, when sugar, butter, ham and bacon was restricted, soon to be followed by meat, tea, margarine, cheese and eggs, and a whole range of goods, not only food, quickly came under control. The Board of Trade instigated a utility cloth and clothing programme and set up the Utility Furniture Scheme, producing durable, attractive pieces at affordable prices.

Householders were encouraged to continue digging their allotments, following the success of the Dig for Victory campaign of the war years. The Women's Institute instigated Operation *Produce* in 1947, with schemes for the production of vegetables, fruit, rabbits, poultry, pigs and more. Pig Clubs – over 7,000 of these flourished during the Second World War; pigs were fed mostly on kitchen waste, but they also had a special half-ration of feedstuffs – and chicken-keeping – which eventually produced a quarter of the country's eggs – proliferated. Bread was at a premium, and the Ministry sought to encourage a National Wholemeal Loaf, and fined those who wasted it, even by giving it to the birds. The popular *Kitchen Front* radio programme broadcast culinary advice to millions while popular magazines, such as *Woman's Own*, *Housewife* and *Good Housekeeping*, were filled with articles on how to combat austerity.

Today, our own cash-strapped times have seen us turn back to grow-your-own and make-your-own and seek new ways to enjoy life inexpensively. Many of us now have allotments, while others have turned over parts of the garden to vegetable and fruit production. We look to cheap ways of making ends meet, of creating tasty meals from fresh, healthy produce – the diet of most Britons, it has often been noted, was rarely as healthy as during the war years and after, when rationing ensured that nutritional advice was heeded – and making use of wild foods for free. At the same time, a growing sense of our environmental tread has encouraged us to repair rather than replace, and not only to Make do and Mend but to Make. Just as in the austerity period, we wish to recycle old clothes into new, to knit and sew, and to reclaim simple pleasures and ways of amusing ourselves that cost little or nothing.

This book gathers together some of the best material produced in the austerity period by the Board of Trade and the Ministry of Agriculture, alongside contemporary advice and instructions from other sources. Of course, a book of this length can only offer a sample of what was produced, that has stood the test of time, but nevertheless it provides a host of timely and time-tried practical tips and instructions that will be useful today.

Growmore Bulletins were issued on all manner of things to do with the garden, from how to make a compost heap to growing small fruits and pickling, bottling and drying fruit and vegetables. There are recipes for jellies and jam-making and old-fashioned tea-time fare. Ambrose Heath tells us what to do with left-overs, while Jason Hill writes about wild food that can be gathered from hedgerow and field.

People were as keen then as now to dress stylishly on a budget, though renovation and making do were to the fore – Princess Margaret, it was noted, appeared in one outfit on three occasions, amended each time. Accessories make all the difference in dressing up an old outfit, and here are instructions on how to make a cloche hat and a knitted jacket and adding a feminine frill to gloves. There are money-saving tips for the home front too – on saving fuel, re-webbing a chair and home-made cleaning materials, as well as easy-to-make home accessories for the carpenter.

And when you've downed tools? Back then, railway-owners promoted the value of holidaying in Britain, and camping and rambling became popular. At home families turned to jigsaws

Poster entitled 'Eat The Basic 7...Every Day' offers suggestions from a 'pie chart' on various types of foods to eat for healthy nutrition, accompanied by the advice to 'Eat a lunch that packs a punch!', early 1940s.

GOOD EYESIGHT PAYS

GROUP ONE

GROUP TWO

ORANGES, TOMATOES, GRAPEFRUIT...
or raw cabbage or salad greens

PROTECT YOURSELF FROM ILLNESS

ILLNESS

GROUP THREE

POTATOES AND OTHER VEGETABLES AND FRUITS
raw, dried, cooked, frozen or canned

HELPS YOU DISH IT OUT

MILK AND MILK PRODUCTS...
fluid, evaporated, dried milk, or cheese

GROUP FOUR

FOR STRONG BONES AND TEETH

PACKS A PUNCH!

and home-made games as well as those 'useful' hobbies that were such a stalwart during the austerity period such as patchwork. Included here too are parlour races and ideas for toys to make and small gifts. There is, after all, fun to be had alongside the frugality.

Part 1

IN THE GARDEN

Dig! Dig! Dig! And your muscles will grow big

Keep on pushing the spade

Don't mind the worms

Just ignore their squirms

And when your back aches laugh with glee

And keep on diggin'

Till we give our foes a Wiggin'

Dig! Dig! Dig! to Victory

FRUIT TREES FOR THE GARDEN

Although your garden may already be well stocked with vegetables, there may still be space to add some fruit trees without upsetting the balance of the vegetable plot, provided plantings are confined to the compact, restricted type of trees or bushes which are easy to handle, give a quick return and take up very little space.

The question of quick cropping is most important, because some kinds of fruit come into bearing much sooner than others. The aim should be to choose those kinds which will yield some fruit in their second year, with an increasingly heavy crop in subsequent years. Of the tree fruits, apples yield the best results the quickest. Pears, plums and cherries take a fair time to come into bearing, since for several years after planting their energy is concentrated on making growth. Apples, on the other hand, can be obtained on dwarfing rootstocks, and with proper treatment should produce fruit in their second year after planting, provided the trees are of the correct age to start with.

FORM OF TREE

The form of apple tree to plant should be limited to the cordon or small bush. The cordon tree has a single straight stem furnished with fruiting spurs along its entire length, and should be used when planting against walls or fences. The small bush tree has a stem of about 20in before branching takes place, and eight to twelve branches grow in the form of a cup, leaving an open centre; this form should be chosen when planting in the open garden. The half and full standards, with their 3- and 6ft stems respectively, should if possible be avoided because they are on vigorous rootstocks, and the trees grow large and come into cropping only after many years delay.

Apples are propagated by budding or grafting scions of the selected variety on special rootstocks. This is an important point, because the rootstock has a marked influence on the growth of the tree and consequently on the age at which the tree will start to bear. If the rootstock is vigorous, growth is also vigorous and bearing is delayed. If, on the other hand, the tree has been propagated on a dwarfing or semi-dwarfing rootstock, growth is less strong and the tree comes into bearing at an early age.

Reputable nurserymen use rootstocks of known habit and which have been classified according to this character. If your garden soil is in good heart and fertile, ask the nurseryman to supply the apples on Malling IX, which is a dwarfing rootstock. If, however, you intend planting on a soil which is light and poor, ask for the trees to be on Malling II, which is a rootstock producing trees of medium vigour.

AGE OF TREE

A cordon apple tree should be at least two or three years old when purchased, since a tree of this age will already be furnished with fruit buds. A bush apple tree should be about four years old. This also will have some fruit buds; but what is more important, the initial framework will have been formed by the nurseryman.

VARIETIES

The choice of variety to be grown is important, because the behaviour of any particular variety varies from one locality to another.

The following list gives a few varieties which can be generally relied upon to do well in most districts, but it should be borne in mind that some may not suit every condition throughout the country.

Dessert Apples	In Season	Culinary Apples	In Season
Beauty of Bath	August	Emneth Early	July–Aug
James Grieve	Sep–Oct	†Rev W. Wilks	Sept–Oct
Worcester Pearmain	Sep–Oct	Arthur Turner	Aug–Oct
†Ellison's Orange	Sep–Nov	Lord Derby	Nov–Dec
Lord Lambourne	Oct–Nov	Lane's Prince Albert	Until March
Cox's Orange Pippin	Nov–Jan	°†Crawley Beauty	" "
Laxton's Superb	Nov–Feb		

° This variety flowers very late and is therefore specially suited for districts subject to late frosts.
† Self fertile.

If there is room for only one apple tree, a variety should be chosen which is self-fertile. Where two or more varieties are to be grown, select those which flower about the same time. Avoid the strong growers such as Bramley's Seedling and Newton Wonder and the tip-bearers such as Cornish Gilliflower and Irish Peach.

WHERE TO GROW

It is necessary to decide upon the best position in the garden for each kind of fruit, for much depends upon whether the position is sunny or shady. Apples, in particular, must have abundant sunshine.

USING WALLS AND FENCES

Cordon apple trees can be planted against the south, west, or east walls of the house, provided there is 6ft of growing height available. If the walls are not high enough for cordon apples, cordon gooseberries and redcurrants, which require less height, should be chosen. Where the height is sufficient, but the site too shady, choose a loganberry. In normal times the first choice for the north wall would be a Morello cherry, but as a quick return is necessary blackcurrants should be selected instead.

Nothing should be done to upset the vegetable garden when planning to grow fruit away from walls. Cordon apples for example, should be trained against the boundary fence or planted in a straight line to form a background to a lawn or border, or to form a division between vegetable and flower gardens.

OPEN GARDEN

A piece of open ground, no matter how small, can be planted with one or more dwarf bush apples, or with gooseberry, redcurrant or blackcurrant bushes. If several rows are planted intercropping with vegetables can be carried out for a few years afterwards. Apples planted about 10ft apart on the square system can have a bush such as gooseberry set in the centre of the square so as to utilize every bit of ground.

PREPARATION OF SOIL

Fruit trees and bushes have to grow on the same piece of ground for many years, so it is essential to give thorough and deep cultivation, although elaborate preparation is unnecessary. The best method is to bastard-trench, breaking up the subsoil as far as possible. This treatment should be carried out over the whole of the area, for any attempt to limit the treatment to the immediate locality of the hole where the tree is to be planted will restrict the free ramification of root growth. This applies particularly to heavy soils; a pocket of prepared soil at the tree site is more porous than the surrounding clay and, in consequence, acts as a sump for drainage water.

SOIL FERTILITY AND MANURING

Generally, the average garden soil is in a good state of fertility, so that manurial requirements before planting should be simple. Farmyard manure is best, but if this is not available decayed matter from the compost heap, decayed lawn mowings, or similar material can be substituted. Whichever form of manure is used, it may be applied between the first and second spit of soil in the operation of bastard trenching.

Cordon apples when planted against a wall call for similar treatments, as the soil in such a position is usually thin and liable to dry out. The border treated should be 3ft wide.

In the open garden, the soil for apples does not require special treatment, and no bulky manure should be applied, since this would have the effect of accelerating growth and delaying fruiting.

PLANTING DISTANCES

Cordon apples are planted 2–3ft apart in the row, and bush apples on dwarfing stocks 10ft apart.

SUPPORT

Trees of restricted habit require some form of support if they are to be trained against a wall or fence. Where the fence or wall has already been wired for the training of shrubs, this will serve for training purposes. Where support has to be provided, special wall nails should be driven into the wall at regular intervals. These nails are provided with an eye through which the wire is run, the wires being spaced horizontally 2ft apart. Alternatively, stout poles 6ft long may be secured to the wall in an upright position, spacing them 12ft apart. Three horizontal wires are run between the poles, the first at 2ft from the ground, the centre one at 4ft while the third is set at the top of the poles.

PLANTING

Planting can be done at any time between late autumn and the end of March, but if at all possible plant in late autumn. Do not plant when the soil is wet and sticky, but wait until it is reasonably dry and friable. If conditions are unfavourable for planting when the trees are delivered, the roots should be covered with soil until conditions are suitable.

Remove sufficient soil to make a hole wide and deep enough to allow the roots to be evenly spread out. In planting cordons it will be found more convenient to take out a fairly wide shallow trench along the entire row. Cut back any coarse or injured roots that may be present on the tree, using an upward sloping cut.

Set the tree in the hole and spread the roots out evenly. In planting against a wall or fence keep the stem about 6in away from the erection. Sprinkle some fine soil over the roots, holding up the upper roots should there be more than one layer, and work the soil into any holes or crevices. When the lower roots are covered tread firmly, and alternately fill in and tread until the hole is completely filled in. Firm planting is essential, but never plant any deeper than the depth at which the specimen was planted in the nursery; this can usually be seen by the ring of soil adhering to the stem. Complete the operation by giving a mulch of farmyard manure or well-decayed compost.

Cordon apples are not set upright but are planted obliquely at a slope of about 45°. This is done to encourage fruitfulness and to increase the length of stem. If the rows run north to south, keep the roots to the south, with the top of the tree sloping to the north. When the rows run east to west, it does not matter which way the slope runs.

Bush apples on Malling IX require staking. Use stout stakes. Drive in the stake about 2ft from the base of the stem, so that the slanting stake rests against the stem at an angle of about 45°, pointing into the prevailing wind. Drive in securely until the top of the stake comes to rest against the stem just below the lowest branch. Wrap a piece of sacking around the stem where it touches the stake so as to avoid chafing, and secure stem and stake with strong cord.

HOW TO GROW
SMALL FRUITS

The small fruits, notably blackcurrants, are valuable sources of the important vitamin C. [...] They are easy to grow. Where there is spare space every garden should have a bed of strawberries, a row or two of raspberries. Gooseberries and redcurrants and whitecurrants can be successfully grown as single or multiple cordons against a wall or fence, so saving space. Trained in this way, they take up very little room. Where space is plentiful, they can be grown as bushes. Blackberries and loganberries can be planted in odd corners or trained with little trouble over fences, arbours or the sides of sheds and garages.

The small fruits, especially strawberries, raspberries and blackcurrants, generally need manure if they are to succeed, but a complete mixture of artificials can be used with good results on gooseberries as well as redcurrants and whitecurrants.

STRAWBERRIES

First-class planting stock is essential. Don't buy stocks if the seller cannot guarantee them free from disease.

You can raise plants at home by letting 'maidens' – first year plants – form up to five runners to each plant and removing the blossoms. Peg down each runner when it has grown several inches, so that the end bud that will form the plant is kept in contact with the soil. An even better way is to peg each runner into a small pot filled with soil. The plants transplant well.

Recommended varieties are *Royal Sovereign* and *Brenda Gautry* (*Huxley*).

PLANTING

Dig the strawberry bed deeply. Manure well and make it firm before planting. August and September are the best months for planting, but you can plant in the spring if you take steps to prevent the plants drying out.

Rows should be 30in apart with 18in between the plants. Plant firmly and keep the crown above the surface. Don't let the plants fruit the first year: but, if required, runners may be taken to increase stock.

Keep the bed free from weeds by frequent careful hoeing. Hoe up to the plants – not away from them.

Just after blossoming, place clean barley or oat straw under the fruit trusses. If birds are troublesome, protect the rows with netting.

After fruiting is finished, clean up the plants and remove all runners. Lightly fork the soil between the rows in the autumn.

CURRANTS

A fairly heavy loam that remains moist and cool during summer is best for blackcurrants and gooseberries. Redcurrants and whitecurrants thrive better on light soils. All will thrive either in the open or in partial shade.

Recommended varieties: *Blackcurrants: Baldwin, Goliath, Seabrook's Black*. The first of these is very good for jam. *Redcurrants: Laxton's No. 1, Fay's Prolific. Whitecurrants: White Dutch.*

Currants are easily propagated from cuttings about 10in long, taken from new growth in September or October.

Trained cordons of redcurrants and whitecurrants are best obtained from nurserymen.

Blackcurrants should be grown as 'stool' bushes, but redcurrants and whitecurrants are best grown as 'leg' bushes. To form a 'stool' bush, all the buds are left on the cutting, but for 'leg' bushes all except about four at the tip should be removed.

Autumn planting is preferable, but currants may be planted in spring. A light mulch encourages rooting and growth.

Plant from 5 to 6ft apart, according to variety – the smaller (*Baldwin*) type of blackcurrant and the redcurrants needing less room. Never plant closer than 5ft.

PRUNING

As blackcurrants fruit chiefly on new wood, they require different pruning from redcurrants and whitecurrants. All, however, should be pruned hard at first to induce fresh, vigorous growth. Afterwards, blackcurrants should have the older wood cut right out and the new shoots left untouched. With redcurrants and whitecurrants the aim should be to produce a bush with a permanent framework of four or five branches, the leaders of which are cut back each year to get strength. All new side growths are cut back to form fruiting spurs at the base.

Blackcurrants need annual dressings of farmyard or stable manure; redcurrants and whitecurrants can do with less, or with artificials.

During the winter, fork lightly between the bushes and mulch the surface of the soil with manure or compost.

GOOSEBERRIES

Gooseberries thrive in most garden soils, and generally the culture resembles that of currants. Although they will do well in partial shade, as well as in the open, crowded conditions must be avoided. 'Leg' bushes are best for the garden. These are obtained from cuttings rooted in autumn. Shoots of established bushes may be layered by bending them down and covering with soil.

If trained cordons are desired they are best purchased from nurserymen.

Recommended varieties: *Careless, Lancer, Lancashire Lad* and *Whinham's Industry* for picking green and for jam. *Leveller* and *Cousen's Seedling* are especially suitable for dessert.

Plant the bushes in autumn if possible and not closer than 5ft apart.

For two or three years prune the bushes hard to form a framework. Afterwards thin out the growth each season, shortening the weak side shoots to form spurs.

Older bushes need harder pruning to keep them fruitful. Over-crowded gooseberry bushes are never so fruitful as those carefully pruned.

Farmyard or stable manure is the best for keeping the bushes vigorous and fruitful, but if you can't get it a complete fertilizer will ensure good results.

Fork lightly between the bushes during winter.

RASPBERRIES

Raspberries are easy to grow if attention is paid to a few simple details. They grow well in cool moist soils and succeed in partial shade as well as in the open. The rows of canes should be tied to a simple support of two wire strands fastened to stout posts. Stout string or cord may be used if you can't get wire.

Recommended varieties: *Brockett Hall*, *Norfolk Giant*, *Lloyd George* and *Red Cross*. As raspberries suffer from virus diseases, take care to secure healthy stocks, particularly of *Lloyd George*.

It is best to plant raspberries in autumn or early winter. Plant the canes in rows 6ft apart with 18in between canes. After planting, shorten each cane to a third of its length to encourage fresh growth.

Each year after fruiting is finished, cut out the old canes. In winter thin out the new canes to a reasonable number and fasten them to the wires with string. Remove the tip of each cane in spring.

Raspberries are shallow rooting plants, so cultivation between the rows should be carefully done. Fork lightly between the rows during winter, and, if possible, mulch with manure to ensure fruitfulness.

THE BRAMBLES

These fruits require an open sunny situation, but can be grown in odd corners, against fences and sheds or trained over pergolas instead of rambler roses. Plant in autumn or winter. Dig the soil deeply and place a little manure below the roots when planting. Prune as for raspberries by cutting out every season the canes that have fruited. All the brambles may be propagated by layering the tips of new shoots when growth is completed.

The best blackberries are *Himalaya Giant* (also known as *Black Diamond*), *Bedford Giant*, *Edward Langley* and *Merton Early*.

The loganberry is a distinct and valuable fruit, and two other brambles, the newberry and the phenomenal-berry, closely resemble it.

The youngberry and boysenberry are hybrid brambles, resembling in flavour and other ways both the loganberry and blackberry.

HOW TO PICK AND STORE FRUIT

he harvesting, and more particularly the storing, of the different fruits are most important operations. The fruits which are to be kept, namely, apples and pears, have to be picked at the correct time and stored under good conditions in order that the varieties will keep until their proper season and so maintain a supply of fresh fruit during most of the winter months.

PICKING APPLES AND PEARS

The best general indication is simply to take a fruit in the hand, lift it horizontally, give a slight twist, and if the fruit is ready for gathering the stalk should part easily and cleanly from the spur. Successional pickings are necessary, going over the tree at intervals of two or three days and removing only those fruits which part easily as described above. Never tug or pull fruits, and always bear in mind that apples and pears gathered before they are ripe will not keep. Use a pail or basket lined with straw for picking, and handle the fruit with great care. Bruised or damaged fruit must not be put into store but should be used immediately.

STORING APPLES AND PEARS

The early dessert and cooking apples will be used as gathered from the tree. Storing applies only to keeping varieties. Grade the keeping apples into uniform sizes as they are gathered, and set them out on trays, shelves, or boxes in a cool, ventilated, but not draughty, room or shed. They should be left for 10 to 14 days to allow the skin of the fruit to become dry. Each fruit should then be wrapped and placed in trays or boxes. Use a thin, oiled paper wrap [such as baking parchment], or if this is not available, soft tissue paper or any other clean soft paper. The best kind of store is one which provides darkness or semi-darkness, a steady temperature of 35–42°F, a moist atmosphere, and proper ventilation which can be adjusted as required. Ventilate the newly stored fruit freely for 10 days and then reduce the ventilation.

It is often possible to convert a room, large cupboard, cellar, or outhouse so that the conditions approximate to the ideal. For example, an otherwise suitable room may be too dry, in which case a large shallow tray of water in the middle of the floor will provide the necessary moisture in the atmosphere.

Where such a store cannot be provided, pack the wrapped fruit in wooden boxes or crates and stand them in a sheltered part of the garden on bricks or boards to prevent them from becoming damp, and to allow a free circulation of air underneath. Cover the boxes with straw, and thatch the top so that rain will run off. It may be necessary to provide some such protection as fine-meshed wire-netting against rats and mice. Alternatively, the boxes can be stored in an outhouse, but they must be covered to prevent draught drying the fruit. Dessert pears should, if possible, be stored indoors; they ripen better at a slightly higher temperature than apples, and do not require quite so much atmospheric moisture. Pears in store have to be inspected at regular intervals, because they ripen very quickly and soon go bad if not used at the right time. Apples also must be inspected periodically, and when storing a note should be made of the season of each variety. If in doubt about the season of any variety, consult a good fruit nurseryman's catalogue.

PLUMS

The best dessert greengages and plums are left until they have become soft or even cracking; the rich flavour will then be more pronounced. Fruit for preserving is best left until it is fully mature, but still firm and not soft; damsons, similarly, are picked when 'firm-ripe'.

MORELLO CHERRIES

These are picked when well coloured but still firm and sound.

CURRANTS

Both red and black are picked when all the fruit on the bunch is coloured. A pair of scissors is useful for cutting off the bunches of ripe fruit, as an inexperienced picker tends to crush the end berries.

GOOSEBERRIES

For bottling and preserving, these are picked when well developed but still green. It is a good practice to pick the large berries for culinary purposes and leave the smaller ones to grow larger and ripen for dessert.

RASPBERRIES AND LOGANBERRIES

These ripen over a period, and therefore successional pickings of the ripe fruit have to be made. For dessert purposes clip the fruit off with the stalk attached, but for preserving pull the fruit off so as to leave the 'plug' attached to the plant.

SOWING VEGETABLES AND CROP ROTATION

Some gardening beginners have no doubt been puzzled by the term 'crop rotation'. It sounds a bit mysterious, but it is really quite simple. And it is the only sound basis for vegetable growing. To be a successful gardener you must be methodical. What does 'crop rotation' mean? Simply arranging your cropping in such a way as to avoid growing the same kinds of crops on any section of your plot one year after another. To grow the same crop on the same ground year after year is bad gardening for several reasons. There is also the risk that diseases and pests will be increased in the soil to attack again the following year.

Rotation of vegetable crops affects the condition of your land in four important ways. It ensures that every part of your plot carries, at regular intervals, crops that require thorough soil cultivation. It helps to maintain the content of plant food and humus in all parts of the plot. Some crops will repay for heavier dressings of fertilisers than others, and some will get what farmyard manure or compost is available. It helps to control weeds, for different crops need different cultivations at different seasons; though weeds may withstand the appropriate cultivations for one crop, they may be kept down by the cultivations for another crop. Finally, it helps to control pests and diseases.

The Ministry of Agriculture recommends a three-year 'crop rotation' for a 300 sq. yd plot. It is not intended that gardeners should follow it slavishly, for what suits one part of the country does not suit another. And people have different tastes in vegetables. The Ministry's plan aims at two important things – crop rotation and a sufficiency of vegetables throughout the year, especially in winter when so many gardens still show the scarcity of crops that results from poor planning.

The right approach for the gardener is, first to find out what vegetables grow satisfactorily in his neighbourhood, and then decide which of them he will grow, bearing in mind his family's likes and dislikes. He should then divide his plot into three equal parts. For simplicity we will call them A, B and C. On section A he will grow the first year potatoes and other roots – parsnips (if his family like them), carrots, beet and so on. On section B he will grow green vegetables – all the cabbage family; and on section C he will grow peas, beans, onions and leeks.

If farmyard manure is difficult to get and the gardener has to eke out the compost we hope he'll make, he should manure each year only the section that is to grow peas, beans, onions and leeks. So in three years the whole plot will be manured.

Now what happens to the plan the second year? He should just move his three groups round. On section A, go the peas and beans, onions, etc.; on section B, the potatoes and root crops, and on section C, the green vegetables.

THESE PLANS WILL GIVE YOU YOUR OWN VEGETABLES ALL THE YEAR ROUND

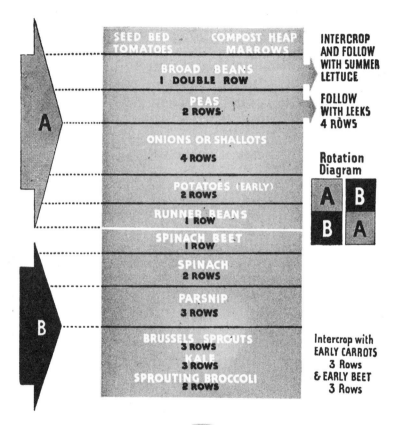

SEED BED — TOMATOES / COMPOST HEAP — MARROWS

A

BROAD BEANS
I DOUBLE ROW

PEAS
2 ROWS

ONIONS OR SHALLOTS
4 ROWS

POTATOES (EARLY)
2 ROWS

RUNNER BEANS
I ROW

SPINACH BEET
I ROW

B

SPINACH
2 ROWS

PARSNIP
3 ROWS

BRUSSELS SPROUTS
3 ROWS
KALE
3 ROWS
SPROUTING BROCCOLI
2 ROWS

INTERCROP
AND FOLLOW
WITH SUMMER
LETTUCE

FOLLOW
WITH LEEKS
4 ROWS

Rotation
Diagram

A B
B A

Intercrop with
EARLY CARROTS
3 Rows
& EARLY BEET
3 Rows

ALLOTMENT
OR GARDEN

PLOT.........45'x30'

APPROX 5 SQ.RODS
POLES
OR PERCHES

COMPOST HEAP · TOOL SHED · SEED BED
TOMATOES · MARROW · RADISH · PARSLEY

MISCELLANEOUS CROPS **C**

DWARF PEAS*
3 ROWS
(2 ft. 6 in. APART)

→ INTERCROP WITH SPINACH (2 ROWS) AND FOLLOW WITH LEEKS 1 ft. APART (4 ROWS)

DWARF BEANS
2 ROWS
(2 ft. 6 in. APART)

ONIONS*
8 ROWS
(1 ft. APART)

→ FOLLOW WITH SPRING CABBAGE (4 ROWS 1 ft. 6 ins. APART)

SHALLOTS
2 ROWS (1 ft. APART)
BROAD BEANS 1 DOUBLE ROW

→ { FOLLOW WITH WINTER LETTUCE INTERCROP WITH SUMMER LETTUCE

RUNNER BEANS (1 ROW)

POTATOES & ROOT CROPS **A**

PARSNIPS
3 ROWS (1 ft. 3 in. APART)

CARROT (MAINCROP)
5 ROWS
(1 ft. APART)

POTATOES (EARLY)
3 ROWS
(2 ft. by 1 ft.)

→ FOLLOW WITH TURNIPS (1 ft. APART)

POTATOES (OTHERS)
6 ROWS
(2 ft. by 1 ft. 3 in.)

SPINACH BEET OR SEAKALE BEET 1 ROW

ROTATION OF CROPS

1st. YEAR	2nd. YEAR	3rd. YEAR
C	B	A
A	C	B
B	A	C

WINTER & SPRING GREEN CROPS **B**

CABBAGE (WINTER)
3 ROWS
(2 ft. by 2 ft.)

INTERCROP SPACE FOR SAVOYS AND BRUSSELS SPROUTS WITH EARLY CARROTS (2 ROWS) & EARLY BEET (1 ROW)

SAVOYS*
2 ROWS (2 ft. by 2 ft.)

BRUSSELS SPROUTS*
2 ROWS (2 ft. 6 in. x 2 ft. 6 in.)

SPROUTING BROCCOLI
2 ROWS (2 ft. x 2 ft.)

KALE
2 ROWS (2 ft. x 2 ft.)

PRECEDE BEET WITH EARLY DWARF PEAS (1 ROW)

SWEDES
2 ROWS (1 ft. 3 in. APART)

GLOBE BEET
2 ROWS (1 ft. 3 in. APART)

ALLOTMENT OR GARDEN

PLOT 90' x 30'

APPROX. 10 SQ. RODS POLES OR PERCHES

TABLE OF PLANTING AND PERIOD OF USE

CROPS FOR A 10-ROD PLOT

Crop	Time of sowing	Distance apart		Period of use
		Rows	Plants	
BEANS (Broad)	Feb–Mar	1 double row	6in by 9in	Jul
BEANS (Dwarf)	Late Apr–Early May	2½ft	9in	Jul–Aug
BEANS (Dry Haricot)	Late Apr–Early May	2½ft	9in	Winter
BEANS (Runner)	Mid-May		9in	Jul–Oct
BEET	(1) Apr (2) Jun	15in	6in (thin)	Jul–Apr
BROCCOLI (Sprouting)	Mid-May Plant Mid-Jul	2ft	2ft	Apr–May
BRUSSELS SPROUTS	Mar Plant May–Jun	2½ft	2½ft	Nov–Mar
CABBAGE (Spring)	Jul–Aug Plant Sep–Early Oct	1½ft	1½ft	Apr–Jan
CABBAGE (Winter)	Mid-May Plant Mid-Jul	2ft	2ft	Apr–Jan
CABBAGE (Cold Districts)	Apr	1½ft	1½ft	Autumn
CARROTS (Early)	Apr	1ft	6in (thin)	Jun–Sep
CARROTS (Maincrop)	Jun–Early Jul	1ft	6in (thin)	Oct–May
KALE	May Plant Mid-Jul	2ft	2ft	Jan–Apr
LEEKS	Mar Plant Jul	1ft	6in 9in	Mar–May
LETTUCE (Summer)	Mar and every 14 days	Between other crops	9in	May–Oct
LETTUCE (Winter Hardy)	Sep	1ft	9in	Spring
MARROW	May		3–4ft	Jul–Feb
ONIONS	Mid-Feb	1ft	6in (thin)	Jul–Jun
PARSNIPS	Mid-Feb–Mid-Mar	15in	6in (thin)	Nov–Mar
PEAS (Early)	Mar and Apr	2½ft	3in	Jun–Jul
PEAS (Others)				
POTATOES (Early)	Mar	2ft	1ft	Jul–Aug
POTATOES (Others)	Apr	2ft	1ft 3in	Sep–Mar
RADISHES	Mar onwards	1ft		May–Jun
SAVOY	Late May Plant Jul–Aug	2ft	2ft	Jan–Mar
SHALLOTS	Feb	1ft	6in	Jan–Dec
SPINACH (Summer)	Mid-Apr	1ft	6in (thin)	Summer
SPINACH (Winter)	Sep	1ft	6in (thin)	Spring
SPINACH BEET	Apr	8in	8in (groups)	Jul–Oct
or SEAKALE BEET				Jan–Jun
SWEDES	End Jun	15in	6in (thin)	Dec–Mar
TOMATOES	Plant end May		15in	Aug–Oct
TURNIP (Roots)	Jul	1ft	6in (thin)	Oct–Mar
TURNIP (Tops)	End Aug	1ft	Sow thinly	Apr

In the third year he should move them round again – on section A, the green vegetables; on section B, the peas, beans, onions and leeks; and on section C, the potatoes and root crops. Then, in the fourth year, he will begin the rotation all over again.

By this simple system you not only ensure that the ground is kept in reasonably fertile condition all over, but it helps you to gauge how much ground you should devote to the various kinds of crops. The rotation can be worked equally well in the garden as on an allotment, but in each case space must be left somewhere at one end (say, 6ft wide) for the seedbed, marrow bed, compost heap and so on.

It is much easier to arrange a proper rotation when starting from scratch; but even a garden that was worked last year could be brought into line by remembering where your crops were last season and trying to plant the appropriate vegetables this year to follow them up.

VEGETABLE SEEDS

Estimating your seed requirements is fairly easy, once you have sketched out a rough plan of your plot and worked out the number and length of the rows of each vegetable you intend to have.

1lb of shallots contains about 25 bulbs, and 2lb should be about enough for an ordinary allotment row of 30ft. Half an ounce of turnips or swedes will sow 100ft. A ¼oz of leek will give enough plants for six or eight rows 30ft long.

One pint of Longpod broad beans will sow a double row 50ft long. One pint of Windsor broad beans will sow 40ft of a double row. Half a pint of French or Haricot beans is sufficient for 150ft. This enables you to sow 2 seeds every 9in to allow for failures.

Half a pint of runner beans will sow one row 50ft long. One ounce of beet will sow 90ft of row. Half an ounce of carrot is enough for 100ft. A small packet or ¼oz of each variety of lettuce should be enough for successive sowings to give summer and winter supplies. One ounce of onion seed will sow 150ft – by sowing very thinly you can make it go still further.

Half an ounce of parsnip is enough for 100ft. One pint of peas will sow 90ft of row – if you sow very thinly; for very early sowings you should allow a little more seed, as some may rot if the soil is cold and wet. One ounce of radish will give you all you need.

STORING AND PICKLING VEGETABLES

A.G.L. Hellyer

B y careful storing and preserving it is possible to extend the season of almost all vegetables (except greens), and in this way increase their usefulness and add variety to diet.

Foods decompose as a result of fungal or bacterial attack, and the methods of storing have consequently to be such that this is reduced to a minimum. Among the few vegetables which will keep for some weeks (or months – depending on the variety) without rotting are marrows, onions, shallots, and root crops generally.

ONIONS AND SHALLOTS

These can be stored in a single layer on well-ventilated slat shelves. Onions can be strung up after plaiting the dry tops together in the manner commonly employed by the Breton peasants. Too warm a place causes shrivelling of the bulbs. They should be looked over at increasingly frequent intervals and any affected by fungi removed immediately, as rot spreads very quickly.

RIPE MARROWS

At the end of the season these have a firm skin and can be kept sound up to Christmas with no further precautions than to sling them in a cool, airy place, each in its own strip of soft material. Only perfect specimens without bruises can be kept. The cut end of the stem may be sealed with wax to keep the pulp from drying out, but this is not essential.

POTATOES

Sound, healthy potatoes may be stored for many months in a 'clamp' or 'grave' out of doors or in a cool, airy, but frostproof shed. To make a clamp, choose a level piece of ground which is well drained and easy to reach in wet weather. If these two are incompatible, build up a suitable level base at least a foot above soil level. Stack the potatoes on this in a ridge or cone. The sloping sides should then be covered with long wheat straw, the stalks running from top to bottom. There must be a layer of straw at least 6in thick all over the pile. To prevent the straw from blowing away, a spadeful of soil may be added here and there, but the straw should be left uncovered for a few days to allow the moisture given off by the potatoes to evaporate. When this has occurred the straw should be covered with 6in to a foot of soil, well smoothed off, to keep out frost and rain. At intervals along the ridge handfuls of straw should be allowed to stick through the soil; these form chimneys for the escaping moisture. The ends of the clamp must also be strawed and covered with soil, and must be made good if the clamp is opened to remove part of the contents.

Potatoes store equally well in sacks in a cool, dark shed, but difficulty is frequently found in keeping a lightly built structure frostproof. Darkness is essential, as the tubers turn green very rapidly in quite low light intensities. A warm store induces sprouting.

Jerusalem Artichokes

These can be stored in the same way as potatoes, but will not keep so long, as they sprout more readily. They need not be lifted until required.

Carrots, Beetroots and Turnips

These may also be stored in clamps. If only a few are to be kept they should be put in sand or fine ashes in a shed, arranged with the top ends outwards. The foliage of turnips and carrots should be cut off cleanly with a sharp knife, but the leaves of the beet should be twisted off, or bleeding results. Care must be taken not to break the skin, as fungi readily attack the roots at such places. Although such a storage place should be frostproof, it must not be warm, or the roots will lose moisture and shrivel very rapidly; sprouting may also occur, especially in the case of turnips.

Runner and French Beans

Young beans of both kinds can be preserved dry. They should be washed and strung as for immediate use, and shredded if large, then dipped into boiling water for two minutes if very young, or as much as five minutes if older. To facilitate the dipping they may be put in the wire basket of a fish frier or loosely tied in butter muslin. Half an ounce of bicarbonate of soda may be added to each gallon of water to help maintain the green colour, but in this case aluminium vessels should not be used. On removal from the water, spread the beans on trays – wire cake trays are excellent – and dry them in a very cool oven till crisp. The temperature should start at 120°F and be gradually increased to between 150 and 160°F. Allow the beans to cool on the trays and then pack into bottles and seal. The bottles must be kept in the dark, or the colour fades. To use, soak the beans in cold water for twelve hours and then boil, with a pinch of salt, in the same way as fresh beans.

SHELLED PEAS

These may be treated similarly, though most varieties do not dry well. *Harrison's Glory* is quite satisfactory, but where a pressure cooker is available bottling will be found more satisfactory.

PICKLING

Preserving in vinegar is an excellent method of using up not only specially grown pickling cabbages, shallots, onions and gherkins, but also green tomatoes, large onions, cucumbers, cauliflowers and broccoli, and also cooking apples. First clean the vegetables thoroughly and then cut them into fairly small pieces. Soak these in brine made by dissolving 1lb of salt in 1 gallon of water. The soaking may continue for anything from 24 hours to 3 weeks according to the vegetable being handled, but for mixed pickles containing the items mentioned above, 2 or 3 days is a good average. After this rinse in clean water, drain and pack tightly into jars, which then should be filled with vinegar (spiced or plain) or, if a thick pickle is required, a mixture of vinegar, mustard and curry powder. Finally the jars are sealed as tightly as possible and stored in a cool, dry place. Vinegar used may be either white or malt, but the latter is usually preferred. Spiced vinegar can be made by suspending in a quart of vinegar a muslin bag containing ¼oz each of cinnamon bark, cloves, mace and allspice, bringing to the boil in a closed saucepan, and then removing from the stove and allowing to stand for two or three hours.

COMPOST – HOW TO MAKE IT

Here is what you can use to make compost and how to make it – in pictures.

What You Can Use

Leaves, grass cuttings, straw, sods, lawn mowings, haulms of peas, beans and potatoes, vegetable tops, hedge clippings, weeds, and faded flowers. In fact, any plant refuse not needed for stock feeding.

What You Can't Use

Cinders, paper, coal ashes, thick woody stems, sawdust, and any materials tainted with oil, creosote, tar or with any poisonous chemical. Avoid cabbage roots affected by 'club-root' disease.

1.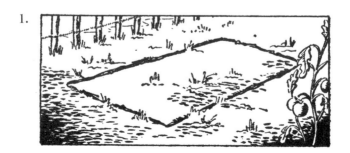

Choose site, in shade if possible, on ground not used for cropping. Width 4–7ft. Length depends on amount of material available.

2.

Cover with layer of vegetable refuse (the more mixed and broken up the better) to 6–9in depth. If dry, moisten and tread down well. If green and sappy, lay loosely.

3.

(*Left*) Cover with 2in layer of animal manure (horse, cow, pig, poultry, pigeon, rabbit) or sewage sludge. (*Right*) If animal manure is not available, sprinkle with one of the special proprietary chemicals or with sulphate of ammonia.

4.

Repeat layers 2 and 3 until heap is 3–5ft high. If more material is to be dealt with, start a new heap.

5.

Sprinkle a little lime, ground limestone or chalk, after every foot or so, or apply a layer of chalky soil about 2in thick. But if using chemicals, follow maker's directions about lime.

6.

When heap has cooled down, turn it over from one end to the other, so that the outside material goes to the middle and that from the middle to the outside.

MAKING THE MOST OF MANURES

A.G.L. Hellyer

I n order to get the best out of any garden it is essential that manures and fertilizers should be used with understanding and not be squandered.

MANURE FROM STABLE AND BYRE

Most gardeners will naturally turn to stable and farmyard manure first of all so long as they can get adequate supplies at reasonable prices. Bulky manures of this type contain nitrogen, phosphate and potash, the three plant foods most likely to be lacking in the soil, but not, of course, in precisely the proportions required by all plants. Consequently it is often necessary to 'balance' these animal manures with appropriate chemicals.

One point in which chemical fertilizers can never compete with dung is in their effect upon the texture of the soil. Animal manures, by virtue of their bulk and sponge-like nature, tend to improve this in a very marked manner, making light soils more retentive of moisture and yet improving the drainage of heavy soils. By encouraging the bacterial and earthworm populations of the soil they also help the gardener indirectly.

POULTRY DROPPINGS

The droppings of all types of poultry may be used in the garden as manure. They contain a higher percentage of nitrogen and phosphates than do stable and farmyard manure, but a very low proportion of potash, so would usually be in need of being balanced by appropriate chemicals [unless used in small quantities]. Being organic they must be decomposed by bacteria before they become available to plants. Weight for weight, poultry droppings are richer than bulky animal manure. Where 1cwt of the latter might be spread on 8 sq. yds of ground without doing any harm, one quarter that quantity of fresh poultry manure would be the maximum dressing desirable. In the case of dried manure the quantity would have to be even more reduced, and indeed such manure is best employed like a chemical fertilizer at 8–12oz per sq. yd. Because of this lack of bulk and also because of its comparatively sticky nature poultry droppings do not improve the texture of the ground like dung.

SEAWEED FOR SEASIDE GARDENS

Those who live in districts in which seaweed can be collected or purchased cheaply have available a valuable substitute for dung. Compared with the latter, seaweed is very rich in potash and almost lacking in phosphates, so, like poultry manure, it is usually even more in need of balancing with chemicals than dung. However, seaweed may either be dug in fresh as gathered at rates of about 1cwt to 8 sq. yds or may be dried and dug in at about 1cwt to 24 sq. yd. The bladder seaweeds and driftweed with long, broad fronds are the best kinds.

GREEN MANURE CROPS

Green manuring consists in sowing some quick-growing crop, such as mustard, rape, vetches or annual lupins, and digging the plants in just as they are about to come into flower. The idea is to add to the organic matter in the soil and so improve its texture and hold up soluble foods which might otherwise be washed out. In the case of lupins and vetches, the nitrogen content of the soil is actually increased, as these plants harbour bacteria which fix nitrogen from the air. The idea is sound, and may be put into effect in early spring on ground intended for late winter greens, etc., or in summer on ground cleared of early potatoes, peas, etc. It is advisable to dust the ground with nitro chalk or sulphate of ammonia at about 2oz per sq. yd as the green crop is dug in, both to hasten its decay and prevent any temporary nitrogen shortage due to the quantity of this element used by bacteria engaged in decomposition. This nitrogen is not lost but only temporarily locked up.

THE HOME COMPOST HEAP

This may very well prove to be the answer to the gardener's problems so far as bulky manure is concerned. A compost heap may be built with any vegetable refuse that comes to hand. Old plants, pea and bean haulm, grass clippings, leaves, straw, hay, green manure crops and even paper and soft hedge clippings may go on to it.

THE GARDEN BONFIRE

Intelligently used, this can be almost as useful as the compost heap, and may enable the gardener to do without chemical sources of potash. Only woody refuse, however, should go on to the bonfire. All green rubbish should be reserved for the compost heap. It burns badly and loses all its valuable bulk. Wood, on the other hand, rots badly, but if burned gives ash which improves the texture of the soil and contains all the minerals that were in the wood, including much valuable potash. Seven pounds of good wood ashes may contain as much potash as 1lb of sulphate of potash, and wood ashes may be applied at the rate of from ½ to 1lb per sq. yd.

HOW TO MAKE AND USE A SEEDBED

S ome seeds are best sown in a seedbed – for instance, cabbage, kales, sprouts, sprouting broccoli and leeks; others, such as the root crops and lettuces, are usually sown where they are to remain. As you may be sowing Brussels sprouts and leeks during March, let us first say something about the seedbed and its use. Here are the essential points:

Mark off a patch about 6ft by 4ft for a 300 sq. yd allotment or garden. Break down all lumps during a dry spell and remove any stones and all roots of grass or weeds. Make the soil firm by treading it as soon as it is dry enough not to stick to your boots. Don't stamp it down.

Loosen top surface by lightly raking. Place short sticks to mark ends of rows, which should be 4ft long across the bed and 6in apart. Stretch line between sticks. Stand on a board so as not to tread ground too hard, and make shallow drill along line with label or stick.

Sow an even single line of seed along bottom of drill. Cover seed lightly with soil. A good way is to shuffle slowly along with a foot on either side of the drill, and without raising the feet slide the soil back and lightly press it. On heavy soil you may find it easier to scatter fine soil into the drill instead. Rake lightly to finish.

SAVING YOUR OWN SEED

Some gardeners like having a shot at something new – seed saving, for example. Those who have not hitherto experimented in this direction might like to try it out. But it is well that they should know that while a few kinds of vegetable seeds can safely be saved by the amateur, others are best left to the experts.

The only 'safe' vegetables for seed-saving purposes are peas, beans of all kinds, onions, leeks, tomatoes, lettuce, ridge cucumbers and marrows.

July is the time to mark the plants you intend to save. The best and easiest way is to tie a label on part of your rows of peas and beans and leave *all* the pods on the plants in that section for seed. Don't pick any at all for the kitchen. If you remember that one-tenth of your pea and bean crop should give you sufficient seed to sow a similar area again next year, you will be able to judge how many plants to leave. Most allotment rows are 30ft long, so of your peas you would need to have 3ft at one end of the row. Runner beans are usually a little more prolific, so one-twentieth of each row is usually enough to save for next year's sowing.

One good lettuce plant should give you all the seed you will need. Mark and label the best plant you have. If the heart is very

Dig for Victory: a woman waters the vegetables on her allotment in Kensington Gardens, London, 1942.

hard and firm, make a cut with a knife in the shape of a cross on the heart. Don't cut too deeply, but just through the first three or four layers of leaves. This will make it easy for the flower head to push its way up. That is all you need to do for the present.

If you spring planted any of last season's onions and left leeks in the ground for seed, they will be coming into flower now. See that the stems, which are very brittle, are tied securely to stakes, but otherwise there is nothing to do to them until the end of September, for onions, and/or mid-October, for leeks.

When your marrows are bearing fruits, pick out one good-sized fruit and scratch the word 'seed' on it with a pencil. When your tomatoes are carrying good trusses of fruits, pick out a good, shapely truss, mark it with a piece of raffia.

The plants that you have selected for seed saving should be inspected carefully to see that they do not develop disease in any way. Leave the pods or fruits to ripen as long as possible. But with lettuces, as soon as you see little tufts of fluff forming on the seed heads, pick them and put them in a shallow cardboard box or a seed-box with a sheet of paper on the bottom. You may have to look at your lettuce plant every day when it is nearing the ripening stage, as a sudden heavy downpour of rain may wash all the seeds on to the ground, if they have reached the fluffy stage. In rainy periods it is best to pull the lettuce plant up when nearing the harvest stage; put it in a newspaper and finish the ripening in a warm room.

HARVESTING

PEAS AND BEANS

If only a pound or two of seed is being saved, leave the pods until nearly dry. The seed at this stage should be firm and tough; pressure with the finger nail should not easily cut the skin but only dent it.

To finish the drying, pick off the pods and spread them in a thin layer in a dry, airy place. When the seeds are quite hard, shell them from the pods and store in cotton or paper bags.

If your space is limited, the seeds may be shelled from the pods as soon as they are taken from the plant, and dried by spreading them in a thin layer on a tray. Move them each day so that they are all exposed to the air in turn.

Onions and Leeks

Onion seed is usually fit to harvest by September, leeks in October. The seed should be black and doughy, not watery, before harvesting. If the stem below the head turns yellow, or some of the capsules burst open, the head is then certainly safe to cut. Cut off the heads with 12in or more of stem attached, and lay them in a sunny, airy place to dry. Place the onion heads in a bag since the dry seeds easily fall out.

Leeks take a long time to dry and the capsules remain tough. The easiest way to deal with very small quantities of leeks is to rub the heads on a fine sieve. If the threshed seeds and chaff are placed in water, the good seeds will sink and the chaff and poor seeds will float. Do not let the seeds remain more than a few minutes in water; dry them immediately by spreading in a thin layer on a dish in an airy place.

Tomatoes

At least 10lb of tomatoes are required to produce 1oz of seed. Remove from the fruit the pulp containing the seeds and put it in a jar to ferment. After two or three days, tip it into a fine sieve and wash it vigorously under the tap; the pulp will wash away from the seeds, which may then be spread on muslin to dry.

Lettuce

Keep close watch for the moment when the seed heads are ripe, since loss of seed results from shattering and from the ravages of birds. Inspect the plants at frequent intervals and pluck off any heads that show a 'downy' formation. This usually appears within about a fortnight of flowering. Finish drying the heads on a tray under cover.

Marrows and Ridge Cucumbers

Leave the fruit intended for seed on the plant until it is fully ripe. The seed should be removed by hand, washed to remove the surrounding pulp and dried in the sun.

Part 2

EATING AND DRINKING

Potatoes new, potatoes old
Potatoes (in a salad) cold
Potatoes baked or mashed or fried
Potatoes whole, potato pied
Enjoy them all, including chips
Remembering spuds don't come in ships!

Potato Pete song

CATERING GUIDE

Good Housekeeping

The following are the approximate quantities to allow per head per meal for family catering.

MEAT AND FISH

Meat:	With bone	4–6oz
	Boneless	3–4oz
Fish:	With much bone	6–8oz
	With little or no bone	3–4oz

VEGETABLES (WEIGHT AS PURCHASED)

Beans (broad)	½–¾lb
Beans (runner)	6oz
Brussels Sprouts	6–8oz
Cabbage	½lb
Carrots	4–6oz
Celery	1 large head for 4–5 persons
Curly Kale	6–8oz
Green (Spring)	8oz
Onions	6oz
Parsnips	6oz
Peas (green)	½lb

WASTE NOT, WANT NOT

PASTE THIS PAGE ON THE KITCHEN WALL—AND TURN TO PAGE 62 FOR ANDRE SIMON'S ARTICLE, "LET'S HAVE A CHANGE"

Remember the stock-pot : In it go any meat scraps, vegetable peelings and the liquids full of precious minerals and vitamins saved from vegetable cookery.

Ask for the bones : You pay for them anyway. Fish bones make a fine court bouillon. The feet and cockscomb of a chicken give a beautiful taste to broth made of the carcass.

FREE CHANGE

The less water, the more vitamins in cooking vegetables. No soda please. And remember, unpeeled potatoes and mushrooms for least waste, most flavour.

Save the fat from soups and stock-pot. Root vegetables, especially turnips, scooped in balls and sautéed golden will taste very French.

Don't despise cheap cuts of meat : Patient cooking over slow heat in a casserole with vegetables achieves succulence and economy ; a pot roast can taste like venison.

Save what's left of us. We make lovely hashes, stuffing for potatoes. Lobster shells are the basis for a heavenly soup.

Give a welcome to the Wheatmeal Loaf. It will keep you fit, and you'll find that it makes lovely toast.

Every drop counts in bottles— rinse them out for desserts and sauces. White wine turned vinegary will tenderise inexpensive meats, give zest to the gravy.

Remember the salad bowl— and that the green outside leaves of lettuce and cabbage are packed with vitamins and minerals—more than the blanched inside leaves.

Peas (dried)	2oz
Potatoes	½lb
Seakale	4oz
Spinach	½–¾lb
Swedes	½lb
Turnips	½lb

CEREALS

Rice (for curry, etc.)	1–1½oz
Macaroni	1–1½oz
Oatmeal (for porridge)	1–1½oz

PUDDINGS

Sponge or suet puddings	1½oz flour, etc.
Pastry (for pies and puddings)	1½oz flour, etc.
Milk pudding, moulds, jellies	⅓ pint milk
Junket	¼ pint milk
Fruit (pies, puddings)	4–5oz of fruit
Custard (as a sauce)	⅛ pint milk

BEVERAGES

Coffee (breakfast)	1 tablespoon
Coffee (after-dinner)	1 dessertspoon
Milk (in tea)	⅛ pint
Tea	1 teaspoon

MISCELLANEOUS

Soup	¼–⅓ pint
Sauces and gravies	⅛ pint

BOTTLING FRUIT

GENERAL PREPARATION

APPLES

Apples should be peeled, cored and cut into slices. If the cut fruit is placed immediately into salt water (1½oz salt to 1 gallon water), discoloration is prevented.

Apple slices may be packed directly into the container and covered with syrup or water, but are better steamed first for about 5 minutes or dipped in boiling water for about 3 minutes, until the fruit is pliable but not too soft.

APRICOTS, DAMSONS, PLUMS

The fruit should be washed in cold water and may be stoned if desired, and the fruit packed whole or in halves.

BLACKBERRIES, LOGANBERRIES, RASPBERRIES

Any stalks and leaves should be removed, and the fruit carefully examined for maggots. If at all dirty, the fruit should be rinsed in cold water.

CHERRIES

Stalks should be removed, the fruit washed in cold water, and stoned if desired.

CURRANTS (BLACK, RED OR WHITE)

The stems should be removed and also the blossom ends if desired. The fruit should be rinsed in cold water.

GOOSEBERRIES

Gooseberries should be 'snibbed' or 'topped and tailed'. When preserved in syrup, either pricking the skins or cutting a small slice off either end when snibbing prevents the fruit from shrivelling.

PEARS

Pears should be peeled, cored and cut in halves or quarters. Placing the prepared fruit in salt water (1½oz salt to 1 gallon water) helps to prevent the fruit from turning brown, but it should not be left long before it is packed into containers and sterilized.

Cooking varieties should be gently stewed until tender in syrup made by dissolving ½lb sugar in 2 pints water. This syrup can be used to cover the fruit in the bottles.

RHUBARB

The stalks should be wiped and cut into even lengths. These may be preserved in water, but if syrup is used this should be poured hot over the prepared rhubarb and left for 8 to 12 hours before packing into containers.

AND PLEASE
DON'T THROW

FOOD

AWAY EITHER

Second World War poster by Fougasse, encouraging people not to waste clothing or food. A sailor on board ship throws his trousers to the winds.

STRAWBERRIES

Any stems and leaves should be removed and the fruit rinsed in cold water.

TOMATOES

Several methods of packing tomatoes are used:

(a) *Unskinned tomatoes.* Remove the stalks, wash the fruit and pack it in containers. Cover with brine made from ½oz salt to 2 pints water. A little sugar (¼oz) may be added to the brine if desired.

(b) *Skinned whole tomatoes in brine.* Blanch the tomatoes in boiling water for about ½ min., then put into cold water. Peel the fruit and pack in brine as in (a).

(c) *Tomatoes in their own juice.* Blanch and peel the tomatoes as in (b). Pack tightly into containers. Stew some extra tomatoes in a covered saucepan with ¼oz salt and ¼oz sugar to each original 2lb tomatoes. Fill up any spaces in the containers with this strained juice.

(d) *Tomatoes in their own juice (alternative method).* Blanch and peel as in (b). Small tomatoes may be packed whole, but medium and large fruits are usually cut in halves or quarters so that they may be packed tightly without air spaces. The flavour is improved if ¼oz salt and 1 teaspoonful sugar to each 2lb tomatoes is interspersed with the fruit when packing into jars. The fruit should be pressed down well, but no liquid should be added.

(e) *Tomato purée.* Heat tomatoes in a covered saucepan, with salt and sugar if desired, until they are soft. Rub the pulp through a sieve, and bottle or can it at once.

FRUIT BOTTLING

The Bottle

Either clip-top bottles or screw-band jars are suitable. The bottles must be washed thoroughly and drained before use, but need not be dried.

Rubber Rings

These are better soaked before use. They should be stored away from the light or heat, and should not be used if they have lost their elasticity.

The Lids

The lids of screw-band jars should be loosened slightly while the bottles are being sterilized, and must be tightened immediately the bottles are taken out to cool.

The lids of 'clip-top' bottles are held in correct position by the clips during sterilization and cooling.

Suitability and Selection of the Fruit

The fruit should be as fresh as possible and in good condition. Most fruit is at its best for bottling when just fully ripe, but it should not be too soft or over-ripe.

Apples. Any culinary varieties are suitable.

Cherries. Black cherries or the red, acid varieties, such as Morello and May Duke, give better results than white cherries.

Currants. Black, red and whitecurrants are all suitable. Large, thin-skinned varieties are the best.

Gooseberries. Gooseberries should be of good size but still green and hard.

Strawberries. The appearance of bottled strawberries is disappointing. Small or medium-sized, firm fruit gives the best results.

A well-prepared bottle should contain fruits of approximately the same size and degree of ripeness, otherwise during cooking some of the fruit will become too soft and broken before the rest is sufficiently tender.

FILLING THE BOTTLES

The fruit should be packed to the top of the bottle and as tightly as possible without damaging it. In bottling stone fruit the liquid should be added after the bottles have been filled with fruit, but in dealing with raspberries and similar soft fruits, it is better to fill about one-third of the jar with fruit, then to add sufficient liquid to cover it, and to continue alternately with fruit and liquid until the bottle is quite full. This prevents numerous air bubbles being trapped in the fruit.

PREPARATION AND USE OF SYRUP

The fruit may be covered either with water or sugar syrup. The latter is preferred because fruit in syrup retains a better colour and flavour, and the sugar penetrates into the fruit during storage. The one disadvantage in the use of syrup is that it may cause the fruit to rise in the bottles, somewhat spoiling its appearance. This, however, is more than compensated by the greatly improved flavour.

The syrup is prepared by dissolving 3lb sugar in 1 gallon water and then bringing it to the boil. This strength of syrup is recommended for all except the more acid fruits (acid cherries, blackcurrants, damsons and loganberries) for which 4lb sugar to 1 gallon water should be used. The syrup should be strained through butter muslin or cheese cloth before use.

The syrup is poured over the fruit when *cool* in methods 1 and 2, but it must be *boiling* for method 3 [see below].

The bottles should be filled to the brim with water or syrup. Air bubbles can frequently be removed by giving the bottle a quick twist after which more syrup may be added if necessary.

Closing the Bottle

The rubber band and lid should be fitted and fixed in position by the clip or screw band. Care should be taken to see that the lid is put on evenly and that the rubber ring is not pressed down below the groove in the bottle when the lid is clipped on.

STERILIZATION AND STORAGE

The following methods of sterilizing are suitable for fruit bottling:

Method 1.

Using a sterilizer. A large fish kettle [a long oblong metal pan] or any container which is deep enough can be used, so long as the temperature of the water in it can be regulated. It must be fitted with a false bottom so that the bottles will not touch the bottom of the container, otherwise they may crack. A false bottom can be made by nailing strips of wood together in trellis fashion, or straw, newspaper or cloth can be used. Care should be taken not to pack the bottles together too tightly, as they expand slightly when heated. The water should be heated very gradually so that it attains the required temperature for the different fruits, according to the following table:

Fruit	Temperature in degrees F. to which water should be raised in 1½ hour	Maintain for: minutes
Apples		
Apricots		
Blackberries		
Damsons		
Gooseberries	165	10
Loganberries		
Plums (ripe, whole)		
Raspberries		
Strawberries		
Plums (halved or unripe)	165	20
Currants (black or red)	180	15
Cherries (sweet or acid)	190	10
Pears	190	20
Quinces		
Tomatoes	190	30

The bottles should be removed from the sterilizer with tongs, placed on a wooden table or board, the screw tops tightened, and allowed to cool.

Method 2.

By this method the bottles of fruit are heated in a sterilizer for shorter periods on two consecutive days.

The bottles should be put in a sterilizer fitted with a false bottom and covered with water as in Method 1. Then raise the temperature of the water to 170°F in ½ hour, and maintain at this temperature for 10 minutes.

The following day the sterilization must be repeated – raising the temperature of the water from cold up to 170°F in ½ hour and maintaining it at this temperature for 10 minutes. The bottles should then be taken out and allowed to cool as in Method 1.

Method 3.

This is a method of bottling stewed fruits or fruit juice.

Stew the fruit in a saucepan with just sufficient water or sugar syrup to prevent it burning. When the fruit is cooked and while still boiling, pour it into *hot*, clean, preserving jars and seal immediately with sterilized lids.

Fruit bottled by this method is likely to become broken, but it is a quick method of preserving fruit pulp, juice or fruit which is to be used later for jam.

Testing the Seal

The bottles of fruit must be left to cool completely before the screw bands or clips are removed, and are usually left overnight.

When cool, the screw bands or clips should be removed and each bottle carefully lifted by the lid. If the lid remains firm there is a good vacuum, but if the lid comes off it means that air has entered while the fruit has been cooling and the fruit will not keep. A faulty vacuum may be due to a flaw in the rubber ring or to a chip in the jar, or the rubber ring may have been pushed out of position when the lid was put on. If the cause of the leak is seen, this should be remedied and the bottle of fruit resterilized.

All jars should be wiped to remove any syrup, and labelled before storing. Screw bands should be dried and only put on loosely during storage. Clips should not be left on the bottles. A smear of vaseline or oil on the inside of the screw band helps to prevent rust.

Storage

Bottled fruit should be stored in a cool, dark store as strong light causes the colour of the fruit to fade. To open the bottles, insert the point of a knife on the rubber ring, and very gently lever up until a stream of air-bubbles enters. It will also help if the bottles are stood in hot water.

The strict rationing of the Austerity era meant that some families relied on extra help in the form of food parcels, such as this one, sent from America in 1946.

SOME CHEAP AND CHEERFUL CHUTNEYS

APPLE CHUTNEY

3lb apples (peeled)
½lb raisins
¼lb onions
¼lb mustard seed
3 pints vinegar

1lb brown sugar
3oz salt
2oz ground ginger
¼oz cayenne pepper

Soak the mustard seed in vinegar overnight. Chop or mince the apples, raisins and onions. Heat all the ingredients until soft enough to press through a colander.

APPLE CHUTNEY (NO SUGAR) ✗

4lb apples (peeled and cored)
2lb onions
1lb dried apricots or peaches
1lb sultanas or raisins
1½ pints vinegar

1 teaspoon ground ginger
1 teaspoon cayenne pepper
½ teaspoon cloves
2 teaspoons salt

Chop or mince the apples, onions and dried fruit, and simmer them with the spices and 1 pint vinegar until tender. Add the remaining vinegar, reboil, and then bottle.

Members of Springfield Women's Institute make chutney at a table set up in the garden of the rectory, August 1941. Bringing the apples, on the right of the photograph, is Mrs Vigne, the leader of the group. Apples, rhubarb and onions were all grown in members' gardens or on allotments.

GREEN TOMATO CHUTNEY ✗

4lb green tomatoes	3oz salt
1lb apples	1 level tablespoon cayenne pepper
1½lb onions	2 bananas
½lb raisins	1lb brown sugar
½lb preserved ginger	1 pint vinegar

Mince the peeled fruit and the ginger. Gently boil all the ingredients except the vinegar and sugar for 1½ hours. Add the sugar dissolved in the vinegar, and boil another ¼ hour.

RHUBARB CHUTNEY ✗

3lb rhubarb	1oz curry powder
1lb sultanas	1oz white pepper
3lb onions	½oz cayenne pepper
1lb brown sugar	1 pint malt vinegar

Cut the rhubarb into small pieces, and remove as much of the skin as possible. Mince the onions and sultanas, place all the ingredients in the pan, and heat gently for an hour, keeping well stirred.

RIPE TOMATO CHUTNEY ✗

12lb tomatoes	Spiced Vinegar:
1lb onions	1 pint vinegar
1½lb sugar	¼oz cinnamon bark
1½oz salt	¼oz whole allspice
A pinch of cayenne	¼oz cloves
¼oz paprika	¼oz blade of mace
2 fluid oz tarragon or chilli vinegar	

Add the spices to the vinegar, bring to the boil, allow to infuse for 2 hours with the lid on the pan, and then strain. Blanch the tomatoes for 1 minute in boiling water, remove the skins and hard cores, cut up and simmer with the chopped onions until a thick pulp is obtained. Then add the other ingredients and the strained spiced vinegar. The chutney should be cooked until it is of thick consistency.

THE MINISTRY OF FOOD, LONDON, S.W.1

FROM WHAT'S LEFT IN THE LARDER

Ambrose Heath

FISH CROQUETTES

Mix together some cold flaked white fish with some cooked oatmeal porridge (twice as much porridge as fish), and add a seasoning of salt, pepper and chopped parsley and lightly fried minced onions. Shape into croquettes, egg-and-breadcrumb and fry.

EGGS OR FISH À LA FLORENTINE

If you have only a little spinach left over, it can be used in this very pleasant dish. Poach the eggs, or poach the fish in the oven. Then lay on a bed of the spinach, cover the egg or fish with cheese sauce, and brown very quickly under the grill.

BREAD PUDDING

To use up stale white bread try this Victorian recipe. Mix together, with a little milk, ½lb of breadcrumbs, a tablespoonful of flour, ¼lb of finely minced beef suet, two whole eggs, 2oz of currants, a tablespoonful of moist sugar, a little chopped lemon peel and a very little nutmeg. Steam in a buttered mould for two hours.

FROMAGE BLANC ✗

Turn 2 pints of thick sour milk into a cheese cloth or piece of butter muslin, and when the liquid has run through, tie the corners together, hang the cloth up, and let the whey drip for several hours. Then put the curd into a basin, and beat it until it is like thick Devonshire cream and quite smooth. Add two yolks of egg, beat them in, sweeten with sugar and serve in a large bowl.

SOME EDIBLE FUNGI

Ambrose Heath

The largest of the recognizable fungi is the *Giant Puff Ball*, which varies in size from a tennis ball to a small football. This should be eaten only when the flesh is white and cheese-like in texture, and then it can be cut into slices and fried or stewed like any common mushroom.

The *Boletus* looks like a penny bun, with its mass of thin yellowish tubes instead of gills, and is the same as the well-known *cèpe*, so much praised by visitors to Bordeaux and Provence where it excels. It is usually either fried in oil or grilled surmounted by a little fat bacon, but in any case it is copiously accompanied by chopped parsley and garlic. The little fawn, bossed *Fairy Ring Mushroom* is known to all, with its tough stem and alternately long and short white gills; the tall *Shaggy Caps*, or *Lawyers' Wigs*, as they are more picturesquely called in some parts, are also easily recognized, but they must be gathered and cooked before the shagginess that gives them their name appears, and while the gills are still pink and the future black-lined umbrellas unfolded. There are, too, the unmistakable *Parasol Mushroom*, one of our largest when fully grown, and the pale *Blewits* with its indelible-pencilled stalk. All these are good when simply stewed with a little fat, for times varying upon their age and size. And lastly, there is the pretty little *Chanterelle,* so charmingly named, and so delightful with its bright frilly gramophone trumpet sticking out of the dry beech-leaves, looking for all the world as though a giant picnic had scattered its litter of orange-peel beneath the trees. Not only its appearance but its lovely smell of apricots, when broken, makes it easy to know. This too, can be stewed, if rather lengthily, in butter or margarine. This recipe, from the *Franche-Comté* is to be recommended. Having prepared the little mushrooms (for the small ones are the best), put them into a casserole by themselves, without any water or fat, put the pan on a low heat, with the lid on, and leave them for a little while until all their moisture has exuded. Then go on cooking them, simmering, until nearly all the liquid has evaporated (but do not let them catch on the pan or brown at all), then add a good piece of butter, and go on cooking them until they are quite tender. Just before serving, pour over them some thick cream, stir all together, and they are ready. This is really excellent, as we proved when living in the neighbourhood of the New Forest, where these little orange mushrooms abound.

MUSHROOM STEW ✗

Experimenters may like to try this Italian dish. Cut the peeled mushrooms in thick slices and put them into a pan with a little very hot olive oil, chopped garlic and a little mint and a seasoning of salt and pepper. Fry lightly for a few minutes, then add some tablespoonfuls of fresh tomato purée, put on the lid and simmer for about a quarter of an hour, when the mushrooms should be done.

WARTIME 'TREATS'

E.P. White

MOCK SAUSAGE

¼lb cold cooked meat

3 rashers bacon

2 tablespoons breadcrumbs

½ teaspoon chopped sage

1 teaspoon chopped parsley

1 saltspoon grated nutmeg

1 fresh egg

½ teaspoon meat extract

1 saltspoon cayenne pepper

1oz fat, for frying

Pass through the mincer the meat and the bacon, the latter slightly fried. Add the other ingredients and mix thoroughly in a basin, adding a little hot water or gravy, if very dry. Mix in the white of the egg and mould into sausage-like rissoles.

Flour the rissoles, dip in the beaten yolk of an egg, roll in breadcrumbs and set aside for an hour to dry. Then fry to a light brown colour in the fat. Drain on paper and serve.

FORCEMEAT BALLS ✗

½lb bacon, chopped fine | 1 egg, fresh
2 tablespoons breadcrumbs | Lemon juice
1 dessertspoon chopped parsley | Pinches of salt, pepper, nutmeg
1 teaspoon mixed herbs

Mix the dry ingredients thoroughly in a basin, add the juice and lastly the egg. If the whole is not well moistened, add a little water. Roll into balls 1in in diameter and bake on a greased tin in a moderate oven for ½ hour. Or, if preferred, fry gently till brown.

These balls make a good emergency meal when meat is scarce. They may be accompanied by vegetables and a white sauce. They also form the basis of a useful curry.

A little chopped cooked kidney or a few drops of anchovy sauce will provide variety. These, of course, should be mixed with the rest at the beginning.

"–AN EMERGENCY MEAL–"

WARTIME WHITE SAUCE ✗

1 level dessertspoon cornflour   ½ pint milk
1oz margarine   Salt, pepper

Mix in a basin the cornflour cold with two tablespoons of the milk. Heat the remaining milk and pour slowly into basin, stirring the while. Return to saucepan with the margarine and condiments and cook for 5 minutes, continuing to stir.

This is the basis of many varieties:
    Mustard, adding 1 level dessertspoon mustard
    Paprika, adding 1 dessertspoon paprika pepper
    Parsley, adding 1 dessertspoon parsley
    Anchovy, adding 1 dessertspoon anchovy sauce
    Chocolate, adding 1 dessertspoon cocoa and same of sugar

"— CAYENNE PEPPER ADDED"

DRYING FRUIT

Drying is an economical method of preserving, as the cost of equipment is small. All that is required is a number of trays made to fit into an oven or any available warm place, such as a drying space over a fire or drying cupboard.

Some fruits, such as apples, grapes, pears and stone fruits, are suitable for drying, but small fruits and berries do not generally give satisfactory results.

MAKING THE TRAYS

Suitable trays are made by nailing together wooden laths into a rectangular frame and stretching wire gauze or canvas over it. The trays may be covered with cheese cloth to prevent the fruit from sticking.

TEMPERATURES FOR DRYING

High temperatures must never be used, and the fruit or vegetables must not be scorched. When an oven is used, the temperature should not exceed 150°F and the door should be left ajar to allow steam to escape. After the oven has been used for cooking, use can be made of the remaining heat for drying by replacing the shelves with trays of fruit or vegetables and leaving all night with the oven door ajar. The trays can be taken out and drying continued on several days if necessary.

DRYING TIME

Fruit should be dried until it is of a leathery consistency but not hard. Large fruits dry more rapidly in halves or slices.

The time required for drying depends chiefly on the temperature, and may be from 4 hours to several days. Drying is quicker if the fruit is turned over occasionally.

NOTES ON PARTICULAR FRUITS

APPLES

Peel, core and cut in slices or in rings about ¼in thick. As soon as prepared, place the fruit in water containing 1½oz salt to the gallon, and leave for 5 to 10 minutes. Spread on trays or thread rings on sticks, and dry until the texture of chamois leather. The fruit should be turned once or twice during drying.

PEARS

Choose fruit that is nearly ripe but not soft. Treat in the same way as apples, but cut into halves or quarters.

STONE FRUIT

Stalks and leaves should be removed; the fruit may be dried either whole or in halves.

NO SUGAR REQUIRED

Solve the sugar problem

by using

TURBAN
DATES

for dessert
and cooking

THEY ARE MORE THAN HALF PURE SUGAR

Try this simple and practical recipe. No sugar required.

"TURBAN" APPLE PUDDING

1-lb. flour. ½-lb. suet. Half a carton of "TURBAN" DATES. 1-lb. apples. Mix flour and suet together, roll out, line a pudding basin. Have the dates ready stoned and cut up, then put a layer of apples and a layer of dates until full up, cover with crust, tie up in cloth. Boil for two and a half hours.

Cut the cost of cooking by using TURBAN MIXED FRUIT for your cakes and puddings. This blending of good fruit goes a long way in saving housekeeping expenses. Choice Currants, Sultanas, Raisins and Peel—all are stoneless, stalked, cleaned, machine blended and ready for use at a moment's notice.

TURBAN MIXED FRUIT

PACKING DRIED FRUIT

The fruit should be allowed to cool for 12 hours before they are packed away. During this time they should be covered with paper or cheese cloth to protect them from insects.

When thoroughly cool they may be packed in paper bags or in jars or tins, but must be kept in a dry place. They should be inspected from time to time, but if sufficiently dried they should keep perfectly.

USING DRIED FRUIT

Fruit should be soaked overnight before use, so that they regain their normal size. To prevent toughness fruit should be cooked in water before sugar is added.

WILD FOODS FOR THE TABLE

Jason Hill

LADY SMOCK *(CARDAMINE PRATENSIS)*

SEASON: spring till autumn

Prolific in damp meadows, where its pale lilac flowers are admired in spring. The leaves are peppery hot and finely chopped may be used to replace pepper in salads, sauces and, with a juniper berry or two if possible, in stews and soups. Young leaves make good sandwiches and can take the place of watercress in country soup. The Hairy Cress (*C. hirsuta*) is similar but milder in flavour and grows in drier, shady places.

LADY SMOCK   HAIRY CRESS

SAMPHIRE

SAMPHIRE *(CRITHMUM MARITIMUM)*

Season: best in May

Common on rocks round the coast except in the north; easily distinguishable by its fleshy leaflets, dull yellow flowers and aromatic, slightly resinous taste. It makes an excellent pickle without the addition of any spice.

SORRELL (RUMEX ACETOSA)

Season: Spring to Autumn; a few leaves can be found in winter

This valuable plant is very common in meadows especially damp ones, and any tendency to mistake it for a Dock can be corrected by tasting it. The sour leaves, young and old, can be used in many ways, for example mixed in salads.

LAVER

LAVER *(PORPHYRA VULGARIS)*

Season: June to March

Laver is a filmy, reddish purple seaweed, common on rocky coasts. It is one of the great delicacies among wild foods and to say that the taste for it is an acquired one is, surely, only to express a diffidence of the unfamiliar. The large amount of iodine which it contains makes it a valuable adjunct to the diet.

LAVER RECIPE ✗

Wash well in several changes of fresh water to remove sand and marine fauna; steep in fresh water for 3–4 hours (not essential), boil gently till quite tender, pour off the superfluous water and beat a little salt into it. The resulting pulp may be kept in jars for a week and served in the following ways:

(a) Add 3oz of butter or a little gravy or meat extract, lemon juice and pepper to 1lb of laver; heat in an aluminium saucepan (it is a tradition to avoid iron) stirring with a wooden spoon or silver fork; serve very hot with roast meat. Laver served in a silver chafing dish with a squeeze of Seville orange juice is a classical accompaniment to Welsh mutton.

(b) Mix with vinegar or lemon juice, a few drops of olive oil, pepper and salt; serve cold on toast. A delicious hors-d'oeuvre or savoury, suggesting a mixture of olives and oysters.

(c) Mix with oatmeal and fry in the form of flat cakes for breakfast.

FISHY FARE

Ambrose Heath

COCKLES

I have found four good uses for cockles, the first and simplest being to use them in place of oysters where a substitute for oyster sauce is demanded. The second is to use them, raw, in place of oysters in that delectable savoury known as 'angels on horseback', though they are not as angelic as the original. A squeeze of lemon juice on the cockles before rolling them in the bacon is an improvement, but be careful not to cook the bacon too long, or the cockles will get tough. *Scalloped Cockles* are recommended by no less an authority than Francatelli, who for some time was head chef to Queen Victoria.

Wash the cockles well, then scald some dozens of them. Strain the liquor into a stewpan and add to it 2oz of margarine kneaded with 2oz of flour, then a little creamy milk, anchovy essence, nutmeg and cayenne. Stir this sauce over

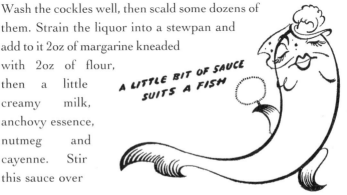

A LITTLE BIT OF SAUCE SUITS A FISH

FISH KEEPS YOU GOING!

A MAN CAN WORK ON FISH!

the heat until it boils, reduce it for ten minutes, and then bind with two eggs and finish with a little chopped parsley. Add the cockles, stir together over the heat for a few minutes longer, then fill some scallop shells with the mixture. Cover with a thick coating of fried or buttered crumbs, brown quickly and serve very hot.

COCKLE SOUP ✗

Boil four pints of cockles until they open, and keep back the liquor. Melt 1½oz margarine, and make a white *roux* with the same quantity of flour. Moisten with 2 pints of the cockle water and a pint of milk, stirring until smooth. Now add some chopped celery, simmer for half an hour and then add the shelled and bearded cockles, chopped parsley and salt and pepper to taste, and cook for a few minutes longer.

WHERE THERE'S FISH THERE'S A GOOD MEAL

PERCH HOLLANDAISE ✗

Get ready three middling-sized perch, and put into a stewpan 2oz of margarine, two sliced onions, a carrot cut small, some parsley, one or two bay leaves, six cloves and two blades of mace. Shake this for 5 minutes over a brisk heat, then add 2 pints of water, two claret-glasses of vinegar, 1oz of salt and a little pepper. Boil for a quarter of an hour, and then strain through a sieve. Stew the fish in this for 20 to 30 minutes, and serve them with a Hollandaise sauce poured over them.

PRAWN PATTIES ✗

An extremely savoury little mouthful. Shell your prawns and leave them to lie for half an hour or so in a wineglassful of sherry with a tablespoonful of lemon juice. Line some patty-pans with puff pastry, and fill these with the prawns (which can be cut in pieces if liked), some chopped olives, a touch of anchovy essence and a little of the marinade in which they were soaking. Put on a lid of pastry, and bake in a quick oven until the pastry is done.

BAKED STUFFED CARP ✗

Stuff the carp with the following mixture: Mix together thoroughly a handful of chopped mushrooms, two chopped hard-boiled eggs, a teaspoonful of parsley, a thinly sliced onion, the carp's roe, a seasoning of salt and pepper and a squeeze of lemon juice. Cook these all together briskly for a minute or two in a little fat, and having stuffed the carp with the mixture, sew it up and bake it in a rather hot oven.

JAMS AND FRUIT JELLIES

JAMS

A good jam is bright in colour, has a pleasant, fruity flavour, and is well set, but not too stiff.

SUITABILITY OF FRUIT FOR JAM

Pectin and acid, both of which are necessary to make the jam set, are present in the fruit, and are richest in fruit which is just ripe. Jam made from over-ripe fruit may not set well.

ADDITION OF ACID OR PECTIN

The less acid fruits may require extra acid. This may be supplied in the form of lemon or other acid fruit juice, or as citric or tartaric acid, added to the fruit before the sugar. Recommended quantities for each 2lb of material, if very deficient in acid, (e.g. pears or marrow) are:

Lemon juice: 2 tablespoons (approximately 1 average-sized lemon)
Redcurrant or gooseberry juice: ¼ pint juice
Citric or tartaric acid: 1 small level teaspoon of either

Lemon, redcurrant and gooseberry juices contain abundant pectin in addition to acid, so that deficiency of pectin is also remedied by their use.

Alternative methods of adding pectin are:

1. Blending with fruits rich in pectin (e.g. adding apples to blackberries).
2. Adding fruit juice rich in pectin (e.g. apple juice).
3. Adding commercial pectin.

SUITABILITY OF VEGETABLES FOR JAM

Some vegetables are suitable as the basis of jam, but acid must be added to obtain a set; and spices or lemon rind are also usually required to ensure sufficient flavour. Carrots, green tomatoes, marrow and rhubarb are the most frequently used vegetable bases.

PREPARING THE FRUIT OR VEGETABLES

Fruit.

Remove any leaves, stems or diseased portions; rinse the fruit in cold water, and prepare it as for other culinary use. Stone fruit may be cooked whole or stoned. If the flavour of the kernel is liked in apricot or plum jam, the stones may be cracked and the kernels cooked with the fruit.

Vegetables are prepared in the following ways:

Carrots. Wash, boil for 10 minutes, place in cold water and scrape. The cleaned carrots should then be chopped, minced or sliced.

Green Tomatoes. Peel, and if large, halve or quarter them. If the tomatoes are put in boiling water for 3 to 5 minutes, depending on their ripeness, and then dipped in cold water, the skins can be removed easily with a sharp knife.

Marrows. Peel, remove the seeds, and cut the edible part into cubes.

Rhubarb. Wash the stalks and cut into 1 or 2in lengths.

SOFTENING THE FRUIT

Before boiling with the sugar, most fruits need simmering to soften the tissues. Sufficient water should be added to prevent the fruit from burning, and it should be cooked slowly until the skins are tender. Firm fruits may require ¾ hour.

Raspberries and strawberries break down easily, and do not need softening in this way.

BOILING THE JAM

Sugar should be stirred into the softened fruit until it is dissolved, and the jam boiled rapidly until the setting point is reached. On no account should the scum be removed until the boiling is finished.

PROPORTION OF SUGAR TO FRUIT

The usual proportions of sugar to fruit in home-made jams are:

Fruits which set readily (e.g. cooking apples, blackcurrants, redcurrants, damsons and gooseberries)	1¼lb sugar to each 1lb fruit
Fruits which set moderately well (e.g. apricots, blackberries, greengages, loganberries, plums and raspberries)	1lb sugar to each 1lb fruit
Fruits which do not set readily (e.g. cherries, pears and some strawberries). *Usually some other fruit juice or pectin is also added*	¾lb sugar to each 1lb fruit

Women's Institute members at a jam-making centre on the east coast of England, c.1940. Large amounts of jam and bottled fruit were produced by the WI to preserve the summer crops of fruit.

For each 3lb sugar used, the yield of jam should be about 5lb if these quantities are used.

Testing for the Setting Point

Begin to test after about 10 minutes rapid boiling, by one of the following methods:

(1) Dip a clean wooden spoon into the jam, remove and turn horizontally until the adhering jam has partly cooled. Then allow the jam to drop from the edge, and if the setting point has been reached, the drops will run together and the jam break away in flakes.

(2) Cool a little jam on a plate. The surface of the jam should set and wrinkle when pushed with the finger, if it is at setting point.

(3) Boil the jam till the temperature reaches 220°F. This method is excellent for jams with the usual proportions of sugar, but should not be used for those with reduced amounts of sugar.

Finishing the Jam

As soon as the setting point is reached, the pan should be removed from the heat and the bubbles allowed to subside. The scum should then be removed, and the hot jam poured into clean, dry, *warm* jars. If the jam contains whole fruit, it should be allowed to cool until a skin is just forming on the surface before it is poured into jars, otherwise the fruit will float to the surface.

The jars should be filled to within ¼in of the top, as the jam shrinks on cooling.

Covering the Jam

As soon as the jam has been poured into the jars, waxed paper discs should be pressed over the surface. The jam may then be covered either hot or cold.

If metal covers are used for the jam jars, they should be heated and put on while the jam is hot. If cardboard discs are used inside the metal covers, they should be sterilized in the oven before using.

Storage

After labelling and dating, jams should be stored away from the light, in a dry, airy store.

FRUIT JELLIES ✗

Fruit jelly should be bright in colour, clear, well set but not too stiff, and should have a good fruity flavour.

Selection and Suitability of Fruit

Most English fruits can be made into jelly, with the exception of cherries, strawberries and pears, which do not contain enough pectin and acid to set into a jelly. The following fruits are very suitable: apples (cooking varieties and crabs), currants, gooseberries, loganberries, medlars and quinces.

Many edible wild berries, such as bilberries and blackberries can be used.

The fruit should be sound, as fresh as possible and slightly under-ripe rather than over-ripe. Jelly made from over-ripe fruit does not set well.

Preparing and cooking the fruit

Rinse in cold water, and remove any diseased fruit. Large fruits should be cut up so that the juice is extracted more readily. It is unnecessary to stem currants, top and tail gooseberries or peel and core apples, as stems and pips will be removed when the pulp is strained.

The fruit should be simmered with water until it is quite soft. This usually takes ¾–1 hour. Juicy fruits, such as raspberries and blackberries, do not require more than 1 pint of water to 4lb fruit; hard fruits and blackcurrants need sufficient water just to cover the fruit in the preserving pan.

Sweet fruits are improved by adding the juice of a lemon or ½ level teaspoonful of citric or tartaric acid to each 2lb fruit while it is being stewed.

Straining the Pulp

Strain the cooked fruit through a scalded jelly bag or closely woven cloth suspended between the legs of an inverted chair or stool. This allows the juice to drip slowly into a basin placed underneath. The pulp may be left dripping overnight, as the juice is not so clear if it is squeezed.

If a fruit press is available, the pulp may be put into the cloths and the juice pressed out. A better yield is obtained by this method.

Second Extraction of Juice

A second extraction can be made from fruits such as apples, gooseberries and redcurrants which are rich in pectin. The pulp should be simmered for another ¾ hour with a little water (about half the amount previously used), then strained as before.

PRESERVES FROM THE GARDEN

"GROWMORE" BULLETIN No. 3
OF THE MINISTRY OF AGRICULTURE
AND FISHERIES PUBLISHED BY
HIS MAJESTY'S STATIONERY OFFICE
PRICE 4d. NET

Boiling the Jelly

The strained juice should be put in a clean preserving pan and
brought to the boil. The necessary amount of sugar should be

added, stirred into the juice until it has dissolved, and the jelly boiled rapidly without further stirring, until the setting point is reached. When the jelly is being tested for the setting point, the heat should be lowered to allow the bubbles to subside.

PROPORTIONS OF SUGAR TO USE

The usual proportion is 1lb sugar to 1 pint juice. If the juice is of poor-setting quality, not more than ¾lb sugar to 1 pint juice should be used.

TESTING THE SETTING POINT

This may be tested in the same way as for jams, but the test should be started earlier, as the setting point is reached more quickly, especially with fruit which sets readily.

FINISHING THE JELLY

As soon as the setting point is reached, the preserving pan should be withdrawn from the heat and the scum removed. The jelly should then be poured quickly into clean, warm jars, filling to within ¼in of the top. A waxed paper disc should be smoothed over the surface of the hot jelly.

COVERING THE JELLY

The jelly may be covered when hot or cold, in the same way as jams. If metal tops are used, they should be put on while the jelly is hot. The jelly should not be tilted while it is cooling.

STORAGE

After labelling, jellies should be stored away from the light, in a dry, airy store.

TEA-TIME RECIPES

Good Housekeeping

PINWHEEL SANDWICHES ✗

Use a new sandwich loaf for these, as day-old bread will crack when rolled. Cut the crusts from all sides of the loaf, and then slice it lengthwise. Spread with butter and a suitable filling such as anchovy paste, and roll up tightly from one long side, to form a roll. Wrap in paper and a cloth, or in plastic material, and if time permits, chill the roll to facilitate cutting, then cut crosswise, giving a Swiss roll effect.

WHOLEMEAL TREACLE SCONES ✗

1lb wholemeal flour	2oz margarine
½ teaspoon salt	2oz granulated sugar
1 teaspoon bicarbonate of soda	1 tablespoon black treacle
About ½ pint milk	2 teaspoons cream of tartar

Mix the wholemeal, salt, bicarbonate of soda and cream of tartar. Rub in the fat, add the sugar and slightly melted treacle, and mix to a soft dough with milk. Roll out about ½in thick, and cut out as required. Bake in a hot oven 15–20 minutes.

Mrs Lillie Taylor of Oldham, Lancashire, at work in the Ministry of Food kitchen, 1942. She was one of 25 housewives chosen to show cookery experts at the Ministry how they varied their rations.

A bolero
adds spice

A bolero can put life, colour, even glamour into other garments which, though good, are inclined to be dull. It can make a simple dress more formal, a dark dress look right on the hottest day.

The bolero here is quickly and easily made. It has new fashion points in the cutaway fronts, winged collar and bold braid trimming. For a summery version linen, piqué, spun rayon or taffetas would be excellent materials. To wear with a starchy white sun-top dress you might choose a vivid print. For warmth, as well as elegance, we suggest fine wool, corduroy or velveteen. Housewife-Butterick pattern 5575, price 3s. 4d., is cut in 30, 32, 34, 36, 38 and 40-inch bust sizes. Short-sleeved version takes 1¾ to 1⅞ yards 35-inch material, long-sleeved, 2 to 2⅜ yards. Coupon on page 121.

HOUSEWIFE-BUTTERICK PATTERN SERVICE

69

Many thousands turned to knitting and sewing during the Austerity period to augment their scanty wardrobes, and found ways of adding glamour through accessories or adapting or adding to existing apparel. 'A bolero adds spice' heralded this advertisement from Butterick in Housewife *magazine in 1951.*

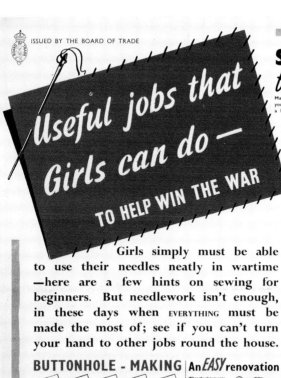

Useful jobs that Girls can do —
TO HELP WIN THE WAR

Girls simply must be able to use their needles neatly in wartime —here are a few hints on sewing for beginners. But needlework isn't enough, in these days when EVERYTHING must be made the most of; see if you can't turn your hand to other jobs round the house.

BUTTONHOLE - MAKING | An *EASY* renovation

Step by Step...

make the positions with pins placed vertically or with running stitch (A): then cut the slit very carefully along the thread of the material. It must be perfectly straight and long enough for the button to pass through easily. Insert needle through the slit and work the cotton from the eye under the point of the needle (B). Draw with an upward movement, thus making a "knot" at the raw edge of the slit. Continue in this way, leaving space to equal the thickness of the cotton between each stitch, until the length of the slit is worked (C) For the rounded end, make overcast stitches (D and E). When the seventh stitch has been made, start to twist, the cotton round the needle again, thus making the first stitch on the second half of the buttonhole. Continue so to the end of the slit, then insert needle through the knot of the last stitch and bring out at base of stitches (F). Work one stitch the full width of the buttonhole (G). Work seven knotted stitches over this stitch (H). Fasten off securely at back. The round end of the buttonhole will take the pull of the button and should therefore be worked next to the opening (I).

When the sleeves wear out of a favourite frock and it gets too short for you, turn it into a slipover to wear with a blouse and skirt. The neckline can be cut in square or V shape as suits you best and the armholes rounded deeply. Outline both neck and armholes first with tacking stitches as a guide to cutting. Allow ¼" for turning and face with bias binding. Dart slightly at the waist, shorten to hip length and hem.

No need for a SHINY SKIRT

You can sponge away shininess if you take it in time, with a cloth dipped in a little ammonia and water. Use about a teaspoonful of ammonia to a saucerful of water. Very often light pressing with a warm iron over a damp cloth is effective if the shiny part, while still damp, is gently rubbed with a brush, preferably a rubber one such as is used for suede shoes.

SNUG S from OLD

Make yourself a pair of cosy slippe your coupons. Besides an old felt h a little strong canvas and some gay

First cut paper patterns—two heel piece for each slipper. Use the diagrams as a g slipper as a guide to size.

Unpick and brush the hat and place a & b. Cut out and, if you like, cut a sin the upper fronts before lining.

Using the same patterns but allowing linings. Any soft material will be suitabl

Join felt heel pieces with a flat seam, ma Press turnings outwards and face with ta tape down each side of seam (6). same way. Then join the linings to the f turning in the lining edges and slip stitch

Cut soles from an old piece of canvas as a Prepare the plaited strands by cutting (d) and plaiting (e). Sew these strands to from outer edge and following the arrow

To join uppers to soles, take the heel turnings. Use two needles (see diagram enter the holes made by the other so even on both sides. Attach uppers in the overlap slightly where they join the heels and centre back.

Cut cardboard 'socks' slightly smaller a layer or two of soft material. Cove drawing this together on the undersid Attach to inside sole with strong adhesiv

TO AVOI
'sea

Preven than cure— lounge about in Change it directly you come in, a when it's not being worn and kee For extra precaution, put a rectang material—the best part of an old dr for instance, across the back. C narrower than the back breadth an side seam. It should be attached at the top and come well below th

MENDING LACE OR NE CURTAINS

It's a simple matter if you ho of similar material large e extend well over the torn par curtain flat on a table with blanket under the place to Dip the patch into rice-wate well, spread it over the ho with a hot iron.

'Useful jobs that Girls can do – to help win the war', a poster produced in wartime on the making and maintenance of clothing, from buttonhole-making to mending curtains and hints on ironing.

...ERS ...HAT

...door shoes *and* ...eral stockings,

A — B — BRIM — CROWN
C INSIDE OF HEEL — D — E
F — G — H

Study your sewing machine

If you have a sewing machine, learn how to use it efficiently. Practise on paper first, without thread, until you get the knack of keeping your stitching straight.

Clean and oil the machine every now and then to get best results. Use only the oil supplied for the purpose and only one drop at each oiling point or point of friction (see diagram). Oiling parts marked with large ring should be oiled frequently —the others occasionally. After oiling, make a

few stitches on waste paper to remove excess.

To avoid breaking needles, do not attempt to pull or remove the material until the take up lever is at its highest point. Don't use too fine a needle for heavy materials.

Missing stitches are due to a blunt or bent needle or to thread that's too coarse.

Puckered seams mean that the stitch is too long for the material or that the tension is too tight.

...on't buy NEW for a

CUSHION COVER

...cushion needs a new cover, make one in patchwork, ...ng odd bits from the scrap bag. Silk or velvet scraps ...uld be lovely and soft—but odds and ends of dress ...ollens will last longer. Trim your pieces to the ...pes you want and tack them to a square of news-...per cut the right size. Then machine or feather ...ch them together, taking care to ...g the joins smooth and flat. Use ... best side of the existing cover ...back the cushion.

WASHING HINTS

Mend before laundering — always make that your rule. Even a tiny run or hole is apt to grow bigger in the tub.

Don't let things get too dirty before washing—the harder rubbing required will shorten their usefulness. Stockings should be washed after each wearing— not necessarily in soapy water.

Always use lukewarm water for woollens, stockings and coloured things. Hot water can ruin them.

Rinse everything thoroughly—soap left in a garment thickens and matts it. Never rub or twist your woollens or rayons.

Hang your clothes to dry carefully—put frocks and blouses on a dress hanger. Spread jumpers and cardigans out flat, patting them to their original shape.

... AND IRONING WISDOM

Don't iron clothes when they are too damp—it wastes heat. Get them nearly dry, then roll up in a towel for a little.

Never sprinkle Rayons. Use a moderate (not hot) iron on the wrong side of fabric.

When ironing sheets, tablecloths, etc., don't press in the creases ; just fold lightly. This will prolong the life of your linen.

Don't leave things damped down and rolled up for too long—this may lead to mildew.

FIX A LOOSE HANDLE

...vided the 'tang' (the bit that ...dle) is at least 1 in. long. First ...le in the handle with a metal ...powder a little ordinary resin ...with it; on top put a bit ...a size of a pea. Heat the ...will melt the resin and ...the resin-filled hole. ...the knife into warm ...Leave for a few minutes. ...m off any surplus resin.

COLLECT WOOD ASH

...the clean white kind. ...to put in a jar near the ...sink. It makes a good ...scouring powder and ...helps to remove stains ...from metal and china.

Care of Brushes

Hairbrushes, of course, need regular washing in warm (not hot) soapy water, with a dash of ammonia. Rinse in warm water, then very thoroughly in cold, to soften the bristles. Shake well to remove as much moisture as possible and stand on end to dry.

Tooth brushes will last longer if washed in cold water every time after use. Always stand with bristles upwards.

Clothes brushes and shoe brushes, too, need washing now and then. Use the same method as for hair brushes. Greasy household brushes call for soda as well as soap in the washing water. Put them away standing on ...not resting flat either on their backs or their bristles.

A SOGGY SPONGE

...calls for a vinegar bath— use only a teaspoonful of vinegar to a pint of water. Rinse the sponge first, then soak it in the vinegar solu-tion for an hour. Squeeze ...clean, rinse again and dry ...outdoors if possible.

S.O.S. for a SCRUBBING BUCKET

An ordinary pot mender from the ironmonger's will stop a leak in a bucket. The discs should be fixed on each side of the hole and held with a screw and nut, the cork disc being placed inside the bucket under one of the metal discs.

WHEN A DRAWER STICKS

scrape its edges well with a chisel. Then rub the trimmed parts with candle wax.

Polishing Pads

for windows and mirrors can be made successfully from worn - out wash-leather gloves. First rescue any bits good enough for elbow patches or cuff-bindings ; then cut open the fin-gers, remove fasteners and lay several gloves flat on top of one another. Stitch a small circle in the centre of the pad to hold it together.

B.O.T. 106.

'The Vegetabull', by The Lewitt-Him Partnership, England, 1941.

Go through your wardrobe

DORA NACHSHEN

Make-do and Mend

BOARD OF TRADE

The need to make-do and mend was well publicized during the Austerity era, with people fixing and patching old clothes rather than throwing them away.

Stuffed Swede. Cooking with limited ingredients became an important skill following the end of the Second World War as nearly all food was rationed. Patsy's Cookery Strip in the Daily Mirror by cartoonist Jack Dunkley, which appeared in the paper from 1946 onwards, featured gardener Mr Digwell.

The Ministry of Agriculture promoted the more unusual types of mushroom to provide variety to the nation's diet in its Bulletin on Edible and Poisonous Fungi during the war and afterwards. Here, left to right are the Chantarelle, the Giant Puffball and the Common Morel. See pp. 78–79 for recipes.

An Austerity era poster form the Ministry of Food designed to encourage people to eat a variety of vegetables to maintain a healthy diet.

Just as today, the health message was just as important in the Austerity period as the need to save costs. 'Don't Forget, Green Vegetables Keep You Fit', a poster by T. Eckersley and E. Lombers, showing a young elephant holding aloft a cabbage with its trunk, was produced by the Ministry of Food in c.1951 to promote the eating of vegetables.

SOME TASTY TISANES

Jason Hill

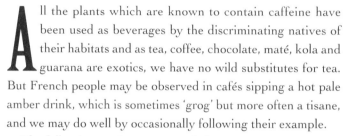

All the plants which are known to contain caffeine have been used as beverages by the discriminating natives of their habitats and as tea, coffee, chocolate, maté, kola and guarana are exotics, we have no wild substitutes for tea. But French people may be observed in cafés sipping a hot pale amber drink, which is sometimes 'grog' but more often a tisane, and we may do well by occasionally following their example.

The following can be recommended:

LIME FLOWERS (DRIED)

About 1 dessertspoonful to a pint of boiling water. Honey flavour.

ELDERFLOWERS (DRIED)

About 3 teaspoonfuls to a pint. Muscat flavour. 1 part of dried elderflowers added to 3 of standard Indian tea converts it into something very like the best Darjeeling or the elderflowers in a muslim bag may be stored with the tea.

MINT (FRESH)

1 part of spearmint (garden mint) with 2 parts of bergamot (*Monarda didyma*) or apple mint or *Mentha citrata* or dried Woodruff (*Asperula odorata*) is unexpectedly good.

The tisane should be made in the same way as ordinary tea; sugar and lemon may be added, but not milk.

Part 3

CLOTHES AND
THE HOME

*'The woman who has learnt home dressmaking under our
direction can clothe herself and her children at less then
half the price she would have to pay in the shops.'*

Women's Institute of Domestic Arts and Sciences
Advertisement, 1948

THREE GOOD HINTS FOR SHIRTS

TO REPAIR SHABBY COLLARS AND CUFFS

Tuck in frayed edges and stitch new folds together. For double cuffs and collars, stitch tape over worn part, and reverse so that tape comes underneath.

TO MEND WORN SHIRT FRONTS

Cut patches of same size and shape from tail or underneath part of yoke. Set edges of patches into yoke seam, and neck-band and into the stitching of front fastening. Replace tail with other washing material.

TO REPAIR SLEEVES

Cut all sleeve patches really large. Patch on right side, matching material.

A CLOCHE AND
A FABRIC HAT

Aage Thaarup and Dora Shackell

TO MAKE SPARTERIE SHAPE

There are two sorts of sparterie* shape. One which is used as a block on which to mould up to one dozen felt or straw hats; the other which is simply the skeleton on which to sew the fabric of a fabric hat.

Both types are designed, shaped and put together in the same way. The difference lies in the fact that in order to be strong enough to steam and shape on to it a felt or straw, the first type will have to be strengthened with extra wire, and coated with spartalac. This is the sort that a model milliner would use in his workrooms.

The instructions given below are simply to demonstrate how a shape is made. The shape could be used for either of the two purposes of a sparterie shape.

Sparterie Cloche

The first thing to decide in making a sparterie shape is the number of

---

* Sparterie shape is a type of foundation material made from willow.

FIG 1

pieces it is desirable to use for that particular design. For this cloche shape four pieces are necessary, a tip, a sideband, a brim and a headband. The brim will be cut on the bias so that it can be given a slight bell shape and also a thick double edge. The sideband is cut on the bias so that it can be drawn in to give a slight waist where it joins the brim.

Start with the brim. Cut a 6in wide strip of sparterie about 2in longer than the outer edge of the brim desired and with ends cut on the diagonal. Damp the sparterie and with the ribbon

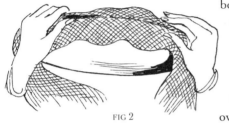

board (a bread board will do) in the left hand, draw the sparterie round the edge of the board so that 1in of it is turned over onto the other side

FIG 2

of the board (Fig. 2). Stretch and smooth out all wrinkles and pin into place with drawing-pins. It may be necessary to run a draw-string round the inner edge of the brim to draw it into a small circle (Fig. 3). When brim is quite dry remove from board

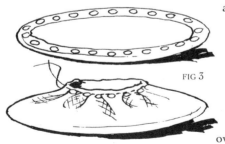

and work into oval shape with slight 'bell' to it by allowing ends to overlap (Fig. 4). When shape and size of brim are correct, pin ends together and oversew. Insert wire

FIG 3

under outer edge fold and stitch to edge, taking care not to flatten soft edge. If a thick edge is desired, pad lightly. Measure head size, allowing 1in for thickness of material and headlining.

Make a securely sewn wire oval this size.

Pin wire oval all round centre opening of brim at points equidistant

FIG 4

from outer edge. Stitch wire securely to brim and cut brim as Fig. 5. Cut a 1½in wide bias strip of sparterie for headband to correspond exactly to size of wire oval and stab-stitch all round as Fig. 6.

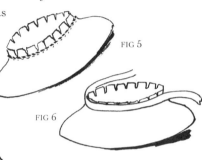

FIG 5

FIG 6

FIG 7

For the crown, cut a 4in wide bias strip of sparterie 3in longer than headband and with diagonal ends. Use 1in of this for overlap at join, the other 2in are to allow for the slight widening of the crown at top.

Join ends of sideband and make a wire oval to correspond with size of top of crown. Stitch wire oval to top of sideband (Fig. 7).

Lay the wired edge of sideband onto piece of sparterie and trace a slightly larger oval for tip. Cut oval tip and join to wired edge of side-band

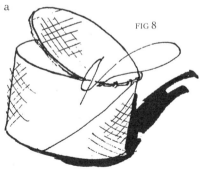

FIG 8

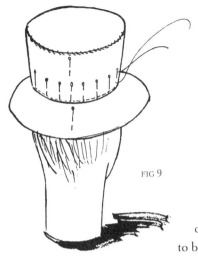

with widely spaced buttonhole stitches (Fig. 8).

Use 'doll's head' to adjust crown to brim. First put pin at centre front and centre back of brim and of crown. Try depth of crown, trim to required depth. Run drawstring through lower edge of sideband and tighten to head size. Press out wrinkles and with pins on brim and crown corresponding, join crown to brim with more pins (Fig. 9).

FIG 9

The shape is now ready either for covering with fabric or for making into a block on which to stretch felt or straw. The crown has not been joined to brim except as a trial with pins, because either to use as a block or as a foundation for fabric, brim and crown must be separate.

TO COVER SPARTERIE SHAPE WITH FABRIC

Starting with the brim, there are two ways in which this could be covered. One is with a bias strip wide enough to double so that it will cover both upper and under brim; the other by cutting a 'V' from each of two circles of material and joining the two edges together at the back of the hat. The nature of the material must determine which of these methods will produce the better result. To make it, in the way first described, with a long strip of bias material it is necessary to have *stretchy* material that will give at the brim edge and close up to a circle at the centre without a lot of gathers. In this case the procedure is simply to make a diagonal join to the strip and run a drawstring round either edge to draw up to head circle. The strip of material must be wide enough to allow a 1in edge of the material to sew to headband. Steam and press out all wrinkles.

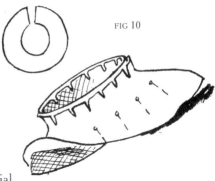

FIG 10

For the second method of covering the brim cut a piece of material an inch bigger all round than sparterie brim. Cut a not-too-big circle in centre and lay material over sparterie brim. Smooth it down all round and cut out 'V' at back to allow material to lie quite flat and to correspond with bell shape. Notch centre opening like the sparterie, taking care not to cut the notches too deep. When 'V' cut-out is joined, ease notched centre opening down over sparterie shape, and pin edges as Fig. 10.

Reverse brim, trim edges to ½in, turn over and lightly stitch edge to sparterie double edge (Fig. 11). Make an underbrim in fabric as upper brim and pin into position, with edge turned under. Slip-stitch with small, invisible stitches.

The crown is first covered with a fabric tip. It should be stretched over sparterie and first pinned, then stitched about ½in below wire top. If necessary cut slight 'Vs' all round to make edges lie quite flat. Make sideband of fabric with diagonal join on wrong side. To ease over crown and to turn in top edge

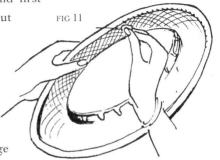

FIG 11

A model shows off her scarlet wool Utility frock by Dorville at John Lewis and Co. Ltd (cost: 11 coupons and 60s), 1943. Her ensemble is complete with the addition of a black wool Utility topcoat by Harella, costing 18 coupons and 90s 9d, perfectly illustrating that chic attire was possible even on the tightest budgets..

a very thin paper knife can be used. Slip-stitch top edge of sideband to tip and turn in lower edge over sparterie.

Ease crown over headband of brim and stab-stitch together. The inside of the crown can be lined with a bias-cut strip of thin silk: a small square of the silk can be stuck to the underneath of tip with millinery adhesive.

To Make Sparterie Shape Suitable for Block

In order to reinforce the brim sufficiently to be able to stretch felt over it, all edges should be strengthened with wire and all surfaces, inside and out, given a coating of spartalac. If it is likely to be necessary to exert pressure on the sparterie shape it will be helpful to stuff shape with cotton-wool or newspaper.

 # 1940S HANDY HINT

Patching a Carpet

CUT AWAY THE WORN PART allowing 1in all round for turnings. Remove the pile from this 1in allowance and fray the threads. Group these threads and fasten with carpet thread on the wrong side. Cut a piece of carpet 1in larger than the hole, matching the design, if any. Remove the pile and fray the edge of 1in all round. Turn these threads on to the wrong side and secure as before. Fix the patch into the hole and stitch at the four corners. Blanket stitch the patch to the carpet, stitching on alternative sides of the join. When finished, press the patch on the wrong side with a warm iron.

Worn carpets may also be repaired by knotting wool through the threadbare backing and then cutting to the length of the existing pile.

A JAUNTY RAGLAN JACKET

Knitting needles will fly like the wind to make this simple stocking-stitch and ribbed cardigan, then with a crochet hook the contrasting borders are worked directly on to the edges.

Materials – 9oz of 3-ply wool, ½oz of the same wool in a contrasting shade; 1 pair of No. 10 and No. 12 knitting needles; a medium-sized crochet hook; 10 button moulds.

Measurements – Length from shoulder, 23½in; to fit up to a 34in bust measurement; sleeve seam, 18in.

Tension – 8 stitches. and 10 rows to 1in measured, over stocking stitch.

Abbreviations – K. = knit; p. = purl; st. = stitch; st.st. = stocking stitch; tog. = together; inc. = increase; dec. = decrease; rep. = repeat; t.b.1. = through back of loops; beg. = beginning; ch. = chain; d.c. = double crochet; in = inches.

BACK

With No. 10 needles and main colour cast on 122 sts. Change to No. 12 needles and work 14 rows in k. 1 p. 1 rib. Change to No. 10 needles and work in st.st. **1st row** – K.

2nd row – K. 1, p. to last st., k. 1. Continue in this way, dec. 1 st.

at both ends of 15th and every following 4th row until 102 st. remain, then continue without shaping until work measures 7ins from beg., ending with a p. row. Change to No. 12 needles and work 18 rows in k. 1 p. 1 rib. Change back to No. 10 needles and st.st., but inc. 1 st. at both ends of 7th and every following 4th row until there are 130 sts., then work 3 rows without shaping.

Armhole Shaping – Cast off 2 sts. at beg. of next 4 rows. **5th row** – K. 1, k. 2 tog., t.b.l., k. to last 3 sts., k. 2 tog., k. 1. **6th row** – K. 1, p. to last st., k. 1. Rep. 5th and 6th rows until 50 sts. remain, ending with a right side row.

Shoulder Shaping – K. 1, p. to last 9 sts., turn. **Next row** – K. to last 10 sts., turn. **Next row** – (P. 4, p. 2 tog). 5 times, p. to end of row. Cast off.

LEFT FRONT

With No. 10 needles, cast on 60 sts. Change to No. 12 needles and work 14 rows in k. 1 p. 1 rib. Change to No. 10 needles and work in st.st. as given for back but dec. 1 st. at beg. of 15th and every following 4th row until 50 sts. remain, then continue without shaping until work measures 7ins from beg., ending with a p. row. Change to No. 12 needles and work 18 rows in k. 1 p. 1 rib. Change back to No. 10 needles and st.st., but inc. 1 st. at beg. of 7th and every following 4th row until there are 64 sts., then work 3 rows without shaping.

Armhole Shaping. 1st row – Cast off 2 sts., k. to end. **2nd row** – K. 1, p. to last st., k. 1. Rep. 1st and 2nd rows once more. **5th row** – K. 1, k. 2 tog., t.b.l., k. to end. **6th row** – K. 1, p. to last st., k. 1. Rep. 5th and 6th rows 3 times more.

Neck Shaping. 1st row – K. 1, k. 2 tog., t.b.l., k. to last 3 sts., k. 2 tog., k. 1. **2nd row** – K. 1, p. to last st., k. 1. **3rd row** – K. 1, k. 2 tog., t.b.l., k. to end. **4th row** – K. 1, p. to last st., k. 1. Rep. these 4 rows 15 times (8 sts.). Cast off.

RIGHT FRONT

Work as given for left front, but with all shapings at opposite edges.

Not a thing to wear!

make yourself a dress
—as you learn
Home-dressmaking

'Eve's age-old apparel problem always troubled me until I saw the window of my local Singer Shop. I joined there and then! By individual tuition, an expert instructress unfolded the secrets

of successful sewing .. The dress I made as I learnt, was acclaimed with wide-eyed admiration by the office . . . Yes, Singer make it *sew easy* to have an extensive and inexpensive wardrobe.'

**learn
home-dressmaking
at your local
SINGER
sewing centre**

SINGER SEWING MACHINE COMPANY LIMITED, SINGER BUILDING, CITY ROAD, LONDON, E.C 1

119

SLEEVES

With No. 10 needles cast on 60 sts. and work in st.st. as given for back for 20 rows. Continue in st.st., inc. 1 st. at both ends of next and every following 8th row until there are 80 sts., then at both ends of every 6th row until there are 102 sts. Continue without shaping until work measures 17½in, ending with a p. row, then shape top as follows: **1st row** – K. 1, k. 2 tog., t.b.1., k. to last 3 sts., k. 2 tog., k. 1. **2nd row** – K. 1, p. to last st., k. 1. Rep. 1st and 2nd rows 22 times. **47th row** – K. 1, k. 2 tog., t.b.1., k. to last 3 sts., k. 2 tog., k. 1. **48th row** – K. 1, p. 2 tog., p. to last 3 sts., p. 2 tog., t.b.1., k. 1. Rep. 47th and 48th rows 12 times. **Next row** – K. 2 tog., twice. Now pass first st. over 2nd st., draw wool through and fasten off securely.

POCKETS

With No. 10 needles cast on 41 sts. **1st row** – K. 1, work twice into next st., k. 17, k. 3 tog., k. 16, work twice into next st., k. 2. **2nd row** – K. 1, p. to last st., k. 1. Rep. 1st and 2nd rows 15 times, then 1st row once. Cast off.

CROCHET BAND

Join shoulder seams, then with the crochet hook, and using main colour, work 1 row of d.c. all round front opening and neck, then join on contrasting wool and work another row of d.c. all round.

To Make Buttonholes – Place 10 pins in 5 groups of 2 at regular intervals along right front from corner of neck to hem, then work another row of d.c. and as each pin is reached work 3 ch., miss 3 d.c. to form a buttonhole. Work 2 more rows of d.c. all round, then fasten off. Work edging in same way round cuffs, but omit buttonholes, then work edging round each pocket, inc. at outer corners to keep work flat.

Buttons

Work 4 ch., and join into a ring, then work 8 d.c. into the ring.
Next round –* 1 d.c. in 1st d.c., 2 d.c. in next d.c.; rep. from *
to end. Rep. this round once. Insert button mould then work
1 d.c. in every alternate d.c. until hole is closed. Make 9 more
buttons in same way.

Making Up

Press work on wrong side with a warm iron and damp cloth,
avoiding ribbed sections. Sew in sleeves, then sew up side and
sleeve seams. Sew pockets to fronts as illustrated. Press all
seams. Sew on buttons.

 # 1940S HANDY HINT

When You've Been Caught in the Rain

Joanna Chase

IF YOU GET YOUR SHOES WET never dry them in front of a fire. Stuff
them immediately with newspaper and leave them in a warm
atmosphere. Don't attempt to polish them until they are quite dry.

All garments that get wet in the rain should be shaken out and
hung on hangers in a warm atmosphere. Felt hats, coats and suits,
velvet or shantung silk that have got spotted by rain should be
steamed to remove the spots. Pass the affected parts of the garment
rapidly to and fro in front of the escaping steam from the spout of a
boiling kettle. This will remove the spots.

WITH LACE AT HAND: A FEMININE FRILL FOR GLOVES

A fairy godmother isn't needed to transform a pair of plain white fabric gloves into a pair, with delicious feminine frills. You can do it yourself in a matter of minutes with enough frilling 2½in deep to go round the wrist of your gloves (about ¼yd for each). Trim the glove to wrist length, or ¾in below gathers, turn in the raw edge and tack frilling in place. Stitch through the centre of the frilled edge. Seam ends of frilling together. Match with other glove.

1940S HANDY HINT

TO SMARTEN FRAYED WRISTS

Joanna Chase

YOU MAY HAVE A GOOD SUIT or frock that is frayed at the wrists. In the case of a suit the frayed edge will be on a fold. Cut it open right round the wrist, and cut away the frayed part, keeping the amount you cut off even all round. Then turn the edges in towards each other, the lower edge slightly beneath the top one, and slip-stitch together. Press over a damp cloth. Where you have to deal with a frayed wrist on a single thickness of material, cut off the frayed part and bind it with ½in wide ribbon velvet to match the frock, or with wide braid in a dark colour.

This photograph shows a model wearing an outfit which illustrates the way in which old clothes can be re-worked and worn as new. The model, seen here leaning on an ornate plinth, wears a black chiffon blouse made from an old dinner dress, a long black skirt made from another old dinner dress bartered with a friend, and a white turban which can also be worn with various daytime outfits.

FIGHTING MOTHS

IN WOOLLENS

Once the moth has got into your things, lose no time in dealing with the trouble – for moths work fast. Woollens and blankets should be hung outdoors for brushing and beating, then soaked for about one minute in water just too hot for the hands to bear – be careful not to change the temperature of the water or they will shrink. This will kill eggs and grubs. You can then wash them in the ordinary way.

IN SILKS

Moth grubs may be found in silk through contact with other clothes that are moth-infected. To get rid of the grubs hang the clothes outdoors, then wash them in fairly hot water.

IN CARPETS

These must be taken up, underfelts as well, and hung outdoors. The boards should be well scrubbed with hot soapy water to which a disinfectant has been added. As an extra precaution or where the carpet cannot be hung out, the affected parts should be pressed with a very hot iron over a damp cloth.

IN UPHOLSTERY

If possible, move the affected furniture into the open air and leave it for several hours. Beat thoroughly. Should the infection be very bad, the coverings must be opened up and the padding sprayed with paraffin, very sparingly. Do not reclose the coverings for several days.

 1940S HANDY HINT

Mending a Table Leg

WHERE A TABLE OR CHAIR LEG has broken diagonally below the level of the rails connecting the legs, a satisfactory repair can be carried out by warming the broken ends of the leg, well glueing the fracture and pressing the two pieces firmly together. Wipe off the surplus glue with a clean rag soaked in warm water and tightly bind the joint with string. When the glue in the joint has set (allow 24 hours undisturbed) remove the string, soak off if necessary, and clean the joint with a wet rag as before.

In cases where the leg has snapped off across the grain of the wood, a temporary repair may be effected as follows:

Turn the table or chair upside down in a level position, warm and glue the fracture as previously described, then press the broken leg very firmly downwards until the fractured ends engage closely. Leave the joint undisturbed for 24 hours, then clean off the surplus

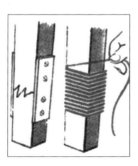

glue. Prepare two tablets of hardwood or plywood about 4–5in long, ½in thick, and of a width equal to that of the leg. Bore a suitable number of holes in each tablet and screw them on opposite faces of the leg. An equal number of screws should be inserted above and below the fracture and no screws should be inserted within 1in of the joint. The edges of the tablets can be smoothed off and the tablets stained if desired.

TO DARN A HOLE

First clear the loops of fluff and broken ends of threads from knitted garments or clip away ragged edges from machine knit fabrics. Always use a darning ball under large holes.

1. Make the darn the shape of the hole.

2. Darn up and down the hole first; work on the wrong side.

3. Choose mending as fine as the material of the garment.

4. Begin a good distance away from the hole in order to reinforce the thin parts round the hole.

5. Space the rows of darning the width of a strand of mending apart.

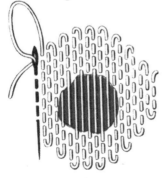
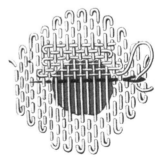

6. Pick up the backs of the loops only unless the material is very fine.

7. Leave loops at the ends of each row and darn so that stitches alternate with spaces between stitches in the previous rows.

8. Pick up the edge of the hole in one row then go over the edge of the hole in the next row. If you have cleared the edges of the hole you will find this will be easy and will make a neater mend on the right side of the garment.

9. Continue the darn over the thin place beyond the hole.

DARNING OVER THE FIRST ROWS OF DARNING

1. Darn over the hole only and about two stitches of darning beyond.

2. Leave loops at the ends of each row and only pick up on the needle the darning stitches.

3. Pick up the alternate strands of mending in first row.

4. In alternate rows, pick up the strands of mending you passed over in the previous row.

HOME-MADE CLEANING MATERIALS

Modern cleaning materials are so cheap to buy that it is usually a waste of time to make all our own as our mothers [or grandmothers] did; but if you have a good deal of leather-covered furniture a preserving and cleansing mixture is really helpful, and as many people still like to make their own scrubbing mixture, furniture cream and brass polish, here are the recipes.*

* Always proceed with care when dealing with ammonia, oleic acid and turpentine, and don't allow the product to come into contact with bare skin.

PLEASE BRING YOUR OWN TOWEL

ISSUED BY THE BOARD OF TRADE

(51713D) Wt 507(?)/6616 100w 3/43 H J R & L Gp 748/6

SCRUBBING MIXTURE

Soft soap	1lb
Silver sand	1lb
Coarse whitening	1lb
Water	2 pints

Put all the ingredients in an old pan large enough to allow them to rise when boiling and stir over the heat until the mixture boils. Then, stirring it occasionally, allow it to simmer until it is a creamy consistency; finally, pour into old jam jars and cool.

FURNITURE CREAM

Yellow wax	4oz
Household ammonia	1½ teaspoonfuls
Turpentine	½ pint
Water	½ pint

Put the yellow wax into a pan with the water and heat until the wax has melted. Remove the pan from the heat, add the turpentine and ammonia, and stir until the mixture is cool. If too thick, add water until the right consistency is obtained.

LEATHER FURNITURE CLEANER

Vinegar	¼ pint
Linseed oil	½ pint

Add the vinegar to the linseed oil, stirring constantly. Bottle, and rub a small quantity on the furniture, using a soft cloth. Finish by polishing with a silk duster.

BRASS POLISH

Whitening — 4oz
Oleic acid — ¼ pint
Paraffin oil

Mix the whitening with the oleic acid and then add sufficient paraffin to make a thin cream which you can apply over the brass.

1940S HANDY HINT

A HAND-SOFTENING MIXTURE

FOR SPECIAL OCCASIONS, when you want your hands to look particularly soft, prepare this simple mixture: equal quantities of olive oil, soap-flakes and granulated sugar. Beat till the soap-flakes are dissolved. Then rub the mixture well into your hands. Rinse in warm water without using soap.

Left: The Countess of Huntingdon pictured gardening in a feature about the importance of looking after one's hands, even during wartime, 1940.

HOW TO SAVE FUEL AT HOME

HEATING

FIRE BRICKS FOR ECONOMY

Put fire bricks at the sides and back of all coal fires. This effects a great saving of fuel without seriously reducing the room temperature. Keep the fire small. Don't put on another lump after 8pm. Go easy with the poker!

USE GAS AND ELECTRIC FIRES SPARINGLY

Replace any broken radiants in gas fires. These are wasteful of gas. Never use two elements in your electric fire when one will do. Keep doors of rooms closed and exclude draughts to maintain the room temperature.

BATHTUB ECONOMY

Limit yourself to one hot bath a week. Use a bowl and a sponge on other days… Never have the water in the bath more than 5in deep.

WATCH THE WATER TAPS

Do not let taps drip. Coal is used in pumping cold water. Have all worn washers replaced. Don't wash or clean your teeth under a running tap. Don't have more water in the basin than needed.

COOKING

GOLDEN RULES FOR GAS COOKERS

Never light your oven to cook a single dish. With a little planning you can easily prepare an entire meal while the oven is hot, as well as a pudding or tart that can be eaten cold next day.

Turn out the burners directly the food is done – it will keep hot in the oven for some time. Always clean your cooker regularly – burners clogged with grease are slow and extravagant. More than half the gas which is used in homes on the gas cooker, is used on the large ring. By using the small ring instead, there is a saving of over one fuel unit in ten, although the job takes longer.

Keep lids on saucepans to contain the heat. Cut down hot meals to a minimum.

WRINKLES FOR WASHING-UP

Use a small bowl…

Heat the water in the oven while it is cooling… Do the whole day's dishes at one time.

Scrape all the plates and dishes before you start. Never wash-up or clean vegetables under a running tap.

IRONING

Electric irons should be switched off for a few minutes from time to time to make use of the stored heat.

To heat up an electric iron for one or two small articles is a most expensive habit. 'Iron a lot while the iron's hot' is the rule.

LAGGING

Lagging is BASIC fuel sense, because it can be done very cheaply or without cost at all, and once it's done it stays done, saving fuel and money year after year without trouble or fuss.

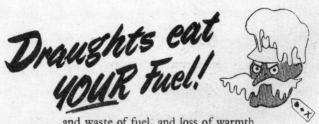
You can buy ready-made jackets for hot-water tanks or suitable materials specially prepared for lagging. These can be obtained from most ironmongers, builders merchants, and general stores.

1940S HANDY HINT

Plasticine to the Rescue

W.M.J. Bath

ONCE, WHEN STAYING WITH A SISTER, I asked what the shapeless mass lying on the draining board was, and was told it was the sink plug! It was simply a lump of plasticine which one pressed down lightly over the grating, and an excellent plug it made, too, easily removable, yet not shifting accidentally. Since then I have found many other uses for plasticine in the home, and a few pennyworth will go a long way. I have caulked the leaking seams of an enamelled tub with it and done similar repairs to the sink where the plaster had cracked away. The plasticine should be smoothed in with a knife, and the surface to which it is applied should be clean and dry. One thing on which plasticine should never be used is anything containing oil, as the oil will dissolve it.

At no cost at all you can improvise suitable material from (*a*) strips of old felt, (*b*) old carpets, (*c*) old blankets or quilts, (*d*) corrugated cardboard or (*e*) sawdust.

Remember that lagging should fit closely and – most important – that it should go on top of the tank as well as round the sides.

Hot-water pipes, both flow and return, between the boiler and cylinder or tank should be lagged, too.

It is a mistake to think that lagging hot-water tanks makes them useless for airing. Sufficient heat will still be available for airing purposes.

'KEEP THE WARMTH INDOORS'

You can have warm rooms with less fuel by letting much less heat escape through roofs, chimneys, and windows.

Badly fitting doors and windows can be made draught-proof by tacking strips of felt or rubber beading round the edges to seal the cracks.

Floors should be fully covered with linoleum or carpet, with an underlayer of newspaper and/or felt. Cracks in floorboards can be caulked with plastic wood from the ironmonger. The gap between floorboards and skirting should also be sealed.

When fires are not used the flue or chimney should be blocked.

Heat rises. It escapes up stairs and through the ceiling into the attic. It can be stopped by laying insulation on the attic floor or between the joists.

 # 1940S HANDY HINT

Re-Webbing a Chair Seat

Carefully remove the covering, stuffing and webs from the seat frame, and lever out the nails with the end of an old screwdriver. Tack on new webbing in the same positions as the old, but do not drive the tacks into the old holes. Each web should be doubled under ½in at one end and fixed with three tacks. To stretch the web, grip the free end with a pair of pincers held against the edge of the seat frame and lever downwards. Drive in three tacks to hold it taut, cut off the web 1in beyond the outer tacks, double the cut end and secure to the frame with two tacks. The webs should be interlaced. ¾in tacks are suitable. Replace the stuffing carefully and refix to cover.

HOW TO MAKE A WOODEN AIRER

Drying or airing clothes in the kitchen is a necessity of most homes, and for such the simple-to-make airer shown in Fig. 1 should commend itself.

The contrivance is simplicity itself, and is made with two ordinary coat hangers and four straight round wooden rods, the latter being slipped through holes drilled in the hangers, as shown in Fig. 2, where three of the rods are in position, and the fourth is shown detached to reveal the catch notch.

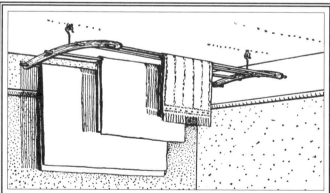

Fig 1: This simple clothes airer made for a few pence can be taken down and put away in a moment when airing is complete.

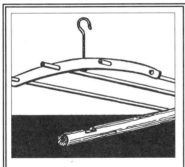

Fig 2: Two coat hangers and four straight rods are the only materials needed for this ingenious but practical device.

Fig 3: Pulleys and lines for airer.

Ordinary ½in diameter white enamelled sticks about 4ft long, or ⅜in diameter ash sticks, can be used. The only work upon them is to round off the ends with sand paper and to file a shallow rounded groove across them about 3in from the ends.

Drill holes through the coat hangers slightly larger than the diameter of the sticks, put the sticks in the holes with the slots downwards so that when the weight of the clothes comes upon them the catch grooves will grip on the bottom of the hole in the hanger, and so be prevented from sliding end-ways.

SUSPENDING THE AIRER

The airer is suspended from the ceiling by the wire hooks which form part of the hanger; these fasten into screw-eyes about ½in diameter driven into the ceiling so that they bite into one of the joists. The position of the joists can be found by tapping on the ceiling, a more solid or dead sound being heard when the joist is tapped. Another method is to drive a very thin steel awl into the ceiling until the joist is found. The small holes left by the awl can easily be filled in with a spot of moist whiting.

Having discovered the joists, drive the screw-eyes into them, slip the rods into the hangers and hook them into the eyes. Any number of these airers can be made and used as requisite, and when no longer required they are unhooked, the rods withdrawn, and the whole stored away in an odd corner until they are again required.

Two women enjoy a meal at a table in a living room set, as part of a display of Utility furniture at the Building Centre in London, 1942. The furniture is finished in light oak.

A HOME-MADE WEATHER VANE

Lucien Ginnett

You need not be mechanically minded to make this ornamental and useful addition to your garden. Only a few oddments, easily acquired from the ironmonger and local garage, are necessary, together with a certain ingenuity – and, of course, accuracy – in assembling the various parts. If you follow the instructions below carefully and erect the vane in a suitable place, you will derive a great deal of pleasure from it.

MAKING THE POST

Take a piece of ¾in gas pipe (one end of which is screwed), 4ft in length. This is the central stem. On to the screwed end a ¾in gas cap is fitted. First weld a ¼in piece of solid round steel, 5in long, to the top of the gas cap. The cap is then screwed on to the 4ft pipe, and four holes, ¼in in diameter, are drilled at right angles, one above the other – the holes must clear each other.

Now take two pieces of round ¼in steel or iron rod, 2ft in length. Pass these through the two holes in the main stem, seeing the main rod is central between the two ends of the ¼in rod.

To the end of each ¼in rod, fix the four points of the compass. These letters, N, S, E, W, are from old number plates, and can be obtained from a garage.

By now the upright post, with the four points of the compass and a thin central pin, is ready.

NOW FOR THE VANE

You must decide what form this is to take. The materials used in the illustration were 4in of ¼in gas pipe, welded to 2ft of ¼in by 1in strip iron, which must carry the actual wind vane as shown – a tree, and the other end pointed to form an arrowhead. The tree must be placed in the same plane as the 2ft of steel strip. The bird, as shown in the picture, is merely for decoration, and serves no useful purpose.

The tree, or any other shape you may choose, is cut from galvanised iron with a pair of tin-snips, and bolted to the end of the 2ft strip.

Before erecting the completed vane, the 5in pin on the end of the main stem must be filed down to be a very easy fit in the 4in tube of the vane.

Obtain a ball bearing, which will drop down easily into the 4in tube of the vane. Fill the tube with thick grease of any sort. This is to lubricate the ball and stop it falling out when you have placed it in the central pin. See that it revolves easily, and the job is done.

Part 4

FUN THINGS TO MAKE AND DO

'We spent many happy hours one holiday composing a family song. Everywhere we went we chanted, tried out new phrases, extended them to form a verse, bringing in the chorus each time, until we nearly drove our grandmother out of her wits… Evenings were the time for genteel walks in the country… We would gather wild strawberries from the banks and sometimes pull bunches of hogweed for grandad's rabbits.'

Jean Grose, *Those Seaside Days*

AN EGG-COSY

L.B. and A.C. Horth

Here is a very simple example of an egg-cosy and a very useful way of using up your small pieces of felt.

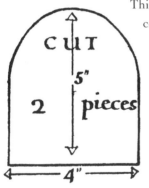

This egg-cosy can be made from any colour felt but it is rather exciting to keep it to just two colours, and then reverse the colour of the front and back. It would be advisable to make a paper pattern. Two pieces of felt should be cut out, each piece should be about 4in wide and from 4½–5in high, as shown in the diagram.

Before joining your pieces together you may like to embroider a small decorative animal on the front of your cosy.

Draw on a piece of paper an animal you would like to see on your egg-cosy, cut out your paper pattern and pin firmly on to the felt. Now cut out the felt

very carefully. Sew on the felt
animal. The chicken on the
front of the cosy shown in the
illustration is embroidered in
chain-and couching-stitch.

Now cut out the decorative
edge for your cosy. You will
need two pieces of felt about
5in long and ½in wide. Cut a
zigzag pattern along one edge. Place these decorative edges on
to your back piece of felt and tack. Then place the front of the

cosy on to this and back-stitch
these pieces carefully together.

It would be rather fun to
make another egg-cosy
to be used with the one
that you have just made,
but this time reversing all
the colours, i.e. red on a
white ground, white on
a red ground.

A TYRE BOATING POOL

Mrs Meeds (P Lewis)

I keep my three little children amused in reasonable weather by placing half an old lorry tyre on their little play lawn. It is an excellent, non-tipable water-way for toy boats, etc., with many other advantages.

It is a great success, especially if there is a sand heap near. It holds five or more gallons of water, which is enough to play with but not at a dangerous depth.

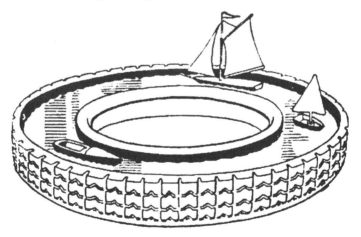

THE ACROBAT

Lynn Miller

This is an adaptation of [that] very old and well-known toy, – the wooden acrobat on strings – a toy which never fails to amuse. The improvement lies in the addition of the stand and the guides (two nails) which both strengthen the toy and enables it to stand on the table while it is being manipulated; as it is thus held steady and vertical, the acrobatics are much more effective. The toy, too, has a much longer life, as when not in use it can stand safely in a corner of the toy shelf or cupboard, instead of being thrown carelessly in a corner with other toys, and broken.

In making a number of these toys for neighbours' children, it was found better to make the acrobat first (Fig. 1), as the slightest variation in drilling the holes for the pivots altered the length of the figure, and the figure when suspended should have the feet just touching the platform. Mark off the five parts on scraps of plywood, and cut out with a fretsaw. Clean up the edges with glasspaper. See that the hands are rather large and wide so that the two holes for the string may be ⅜in apart. The wider apart they are the better the figure works, as the leverage on the string is greater. Mark off, and drill all the pivot and string holes cleanly with a $\frac{1}{16}$in drill. It is best at this stage to paint the parts of the figure in bright colours, and allow to dry thoroughly before pivoting.

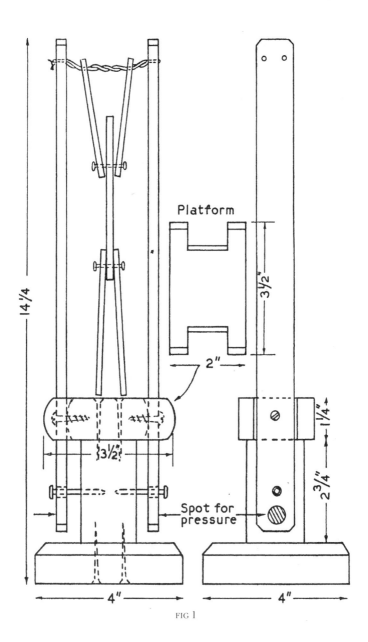

Platform

14¼

3½"

2"

3½"

1¼"

2¾"

Spot for pressure

4"

4"

FIG 1

148

The pivots for the tumbler's joints may be made either as in Sketch 'C' or Sketch 'D' [see following page]. For 'C' the wire should be not more than $\frac{1}{32}$in thick (gauge 18 to 20). Take a 2¼in length, and with round-nosed pliers form an eye at one end, and then square the wire at right angles as shown. Pass the wire through the shoulder holes of one arm, then the body, then the other arm, and form an eye on the projecting end. Press it flat, but see that the arms move freely. Do similarly with the legs. 'D' is used when the wire is very thin.

For the stand, the base is 4in square and 1in thick. On the centre of this is nailed and glued a piece 2¾in long x 1½in × 1½in in section.

The platform is 3½in × 2in × 1¼in cut to the shape indicated (Fig. 1). Give the end faces inside the notches a good rounding off with chisel and file, so that the two uprights will easily rock when pivoted with the 1in round-headed screws. The uprights should be 13in × 1in × ¼in and free from any weakness or defect, as considerable pressure is sometimes used. The two $\frac{1}{16}$in holes at the top should be at least ⅜in to ½in apart, and not too near the ends (to avoid splitting). The easiest way to fix the cord is to lay the stand flat on the table, and arrange the tumbler *upside down*, with the hands opposite the holes in the uprights, and the body stretched away from them, as shown in the side Sketch 'A'.

Lace the two ends of the cord through the two holes in the nearest upright, then *straight through* (no twist) the hand. Then give the cords two twists, and push them through the two holes in the other hand, and *straight through* the second upright. Pull gently to tighten the cord, and tie the ends together. When the apparatus is stood on its base, the acrobat will, of course, hang downwards and the cords between the hands and the uprights will then be crossed as required, and as shown at 'B'. Pressure

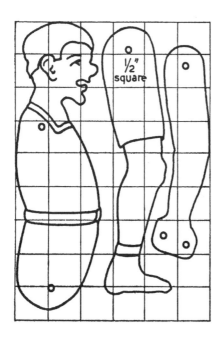

½" square

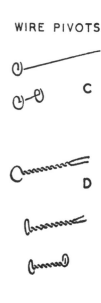

C

D

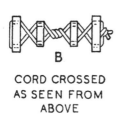

B

CORD CROSSED
AS SEEN FROM
ABOVE

ARRANGING
THE CORD

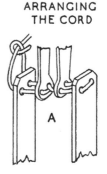

A

with finger and thumb on the spots indicated will cause the uprights to stretch the cord, and the acrobat will perform wonderfully the queerest antics.

PUPPETS MADE FROM WASTE MATERIALS

Margaret Beresford

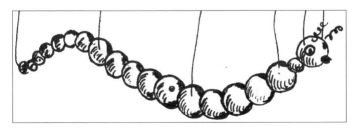

STOCKING

1. Snakes and reptiles can be made from old stockings. Put the hand into the toe of the stocking, stretch the fingers and draw them together to a point to make a snaky head. Use old beads or buttons for the eyes and decorate the stocking with sequins or gilt paint.

2. Cotton reels joined together make a centipede, with springs fixed for feet; but small balls are more satisfactory.

HALF CORK

OLD BOX

SPRINGS

3. Fascinating odd figures can be made by using small discarded boxes for bodies and heads. Corks stuck to the heads make good noses.

Useful Tips

When painting heads, if possible put the puppets on the stage with the stage lights, walk about 20ft away and see if all the features carry.

A pure white skin looks ghastly, but can be used for a ghost or a clown.

Unity should be preserved in puppets. Do not use 24in puppets with 16in ones. Also try not to use wooden puppets with cloth ones unless striving for some definite effect.

Necks can be disguised with chamois leather or flesh coloured silk. Always exaggerate the size of head, hands and feet.

When dressing a puppet it is best to sew or tack the costume on to the puppet piece by piece. For instance, put on the sleeves first, then the bodice, then the skirt and sew together.

A ROCKING-HORSE MADE FROM COATHANGERS

The fascinating pattern made on the carpet by a group of coathangers, carelessly dropped, led to the idea for this simple but good-looking toy. Children will love it because the rider comes off his horse and the horse really does rock.

Materials you'll want for the horse: five coathangers, two nuts and bolts ³⁄₃₂in by 2in; four washers; scraps of leather for mane and tail; two 4in lengths of ¼in dowel; liquid glue; plastic wood; glasspaper; brush and blue, pink, black and white enamels. For the rider: two coathangers; two nuts and bolts ³⁄₃₂in by 2in; twelve washers; large wooden bead for head; cotton-reel for hat; 2in length of ⅛in dowel. Tools for the job: drill with ³⁄₃₂in and ¼in bits; fine gimlet; hacksaw; penknife.

Remove all hooks from hangers and fill in holes with plastic wood. Take two matching hangers for rockers and drill ¼in hole, 2½in in from each end.

Cut four 6in pieces from hangers for legs. The horse's body is made from two pieces, one 3½in long, second 3½in, plus width of hanger (these were ¾in wide, second piece would therefore measure 3½in plus ¾in).

Glue these two pieces together, curved edge to the top, tail ends together.

The neck is two 4¾in pieces; the head one 2¾in piece and another 2¾in less the width of a hanger. Glue two heads together, curves to top, noses parallel.

Cut a leather fringe 1in wide, 5½in long for mane. Glue one piece of neck to head and body, glue mane to this then glue on second neck piece to fit flush against shorter pieces on head and body. Fill joins with plastic wood. Drill hole for tail and stuff and glue in tassel of fringe 1½in wide by 2½in.

Ears are two petal-shaped pieces each on a tiny stem cut from curved part of hanger and glued into two gimlet holes. Smooth over with glasspaper.

Drill ³⁄₃₂in holes in body and top of legs and ¼in hole in each hoof. Paint body and legs blue with black hoofs. When dry join legs to body with nuts bolts and washers. Saw off screws close to bolts and go over them with paint. Push dowels through legs and glue into rocker holes.

The Rider: Legs are two pieces of coathanger 4in long; arms two pieces 3in long; body two pieces 3in long glued together. Fill hole in cotton-reel with plastic wood and push dowel through.

Paint the cotton-reel black and head bead white. When paint is dry thread the bead on to dowel and glue dowel end into gimlet hole in the neck. Drill ³⁄₃₂in holes through arm and leg tops and body.

Join legs and arms to body with nuts, bolts and washers – three washers between legs and body, one washer between arms and body. Paint the rider pink with black 'high boots'.

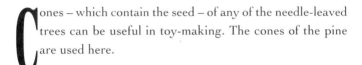

TWO PINE-CONE TOYS

Lynn Miller

ones – which contain the seed – of any of the needle-leaved trees can be useful in toy-making. The cones of the pine are used here.

SWINGING BIRD

Take a piece of straight wire ¹⁄₁₆in thick and 11in long, and spear-point both ends. On one end rivet a head made from ½in dowel. Bore a hole through a suitable cone and thread the wire through, pushing the cone right up to the head. For the legs take a piece of wire 3in long, and bend it double at the centre. Place this against the long wire, with the bend about 1½in from the head, i.e. as close to the cone as possible, and strongly solder it there. The cone can now be pulled down as far as it will come and then the neck may be bent to suitable shape. Open out the legs slightly and bend the extremities, as shown, for the feet. In order to balance the bird, fix at the other extreme end of the long wire a solid but small unopened cone. The feet may be hooked on the edge of a tall vase, a gas bracket, or a stretched string. Paint it in varied colours.

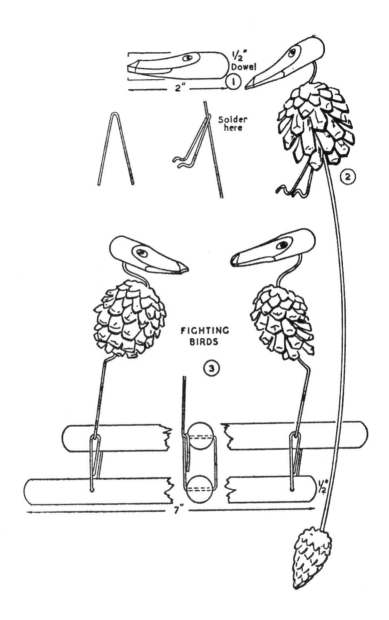

½" Dowel

2"

①

Solder here

②

FIGHTING BIRDS

③

7"

½"

FIGHTING BIRDS

First prepare the heads and cones as before, but the wires should each be 9in long. In this case spear-point only one end of each wire, and rivet the heads on them. Thread a suitable cone on each wire and bend the neck and knees. Now prepare two pieces of ½in dowel each 7in long. Bore holes through for the wires ¾in from one end and 1½in from the other. At a point 4in from the bottom ends of the wires make a square bend with the pliers. Thread each wire through a hole in the top dowel, as shown in the drawing. Pull the wires tight against the dowel, and bend both squarely downwards. At 1in downwards make a third square bend in the opposite direction, and push the wires through the second dowel arranged in the reverse direction, i.e. with the handle end reversed. Hold the two dowels firmly, and bend both wires squarely and sharply upwards, then bend the ends over the inside of the leg wires as shown, and nip them in with the pliers. Try the toy out by holding a dowel in each hand and moving them in opposite directions. The birds should appear to peck at one another, but the wires and heads may need some little adjustment to make them thoroughly effective. If all's well, paint it in bright colours to your own satisfaction.

GLOVE PUPPETS FOR YOUNG CHILDREN

Margaret Beresford

TYPE I

MATERIALS:

Rubber ball, potato, apple, carrot, turnip, or any such similar article. Piece of cloth or small handkerchief.

METHOD:

1. Make holes for eyes, nose and mouth or paint these features on whatever article is used (*e.g.* ball).

2. Cut a hole at the base of the ball to fit the first finger.

3. Place the handkerchief over the first finger, and slip it into the hole in the ball. [See diagrams.]

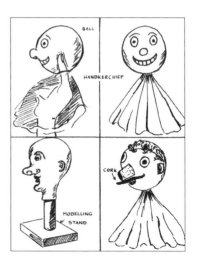

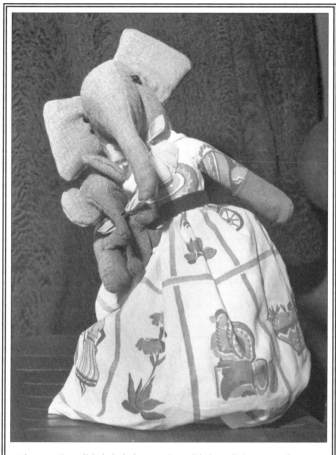

A home-made stuffed cloth elephant mother and baby made in wartime from leftover scraps of fabric and stuffed with cotton waste and old stockings.

A useful modelling stand can be made (by an adult) of ¾in or 1in dowel set in a wooden base. If the stand can be constructed to revolve so much the better.

TYPE II

MATERIALS:

Newspaper, cold water, paste.

METHOD:

1. Let the children tear up the newspaper into small pieces, and put them into a bowl of water. The more the children play with the paper in the water the more the paper will get broken up. Let the paper soak all night.

2. Squeeze out all the water and mix the pulp with paste. Add the paste a little at a time in order to get the right consistency. The children will enjoy mixing the paper and paste with their hands.

3. The pulp can now be made into a ball for a head. Remember to make a hole at the base to fit the first finger before the head is dry. The head may take about two days to dry.

PATCHWORK

L.B. and A.C. Horth

P atchwork is a method of using up odd scraps of material by stitching them together in a variety of patterns made by combining simple shapes such as squares, triangles, and the like. So here is a chance to clear out that over-stuffed bag of odds and ends *too* nice to throw away!

There are many shapes that can be cut for patchwork, but because it is necessary to be very accurate at the corners it will be easier for you to start with quite simple ones. Always keep to one kind of material, such as all silk, or all cotton.

To make a patchwork needlecase you will need a stiff paper template for each piece [Fig 1] – not too stiff though, because the needle has to be able to pass through it easily. Cut out as many pieces as you will need before you start.

When you have done this, place one of your templates on a piece of material, allowing ½in all round for turning. Now bring the ½in turning back over the paper, and tack through both it and the material making sure that the corners are neat and fitting [Fig 2]. When you have done this and you have several of the templates ready, join them together by over-sewing as shown in Fig. 3.

PATCHWORK

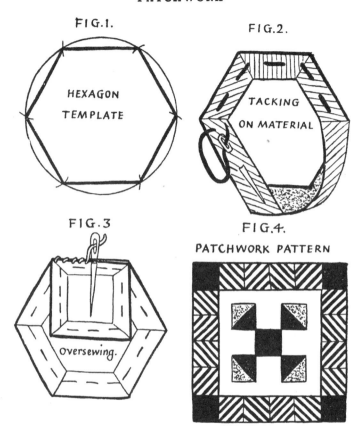

FIG.1.

HEXAGON
TEMPLATE

FIG.2.

TACKING
ON MATERIAL

FIG.3

Oversewing.

FIG.4.

PATCHWORK PATTERN

With all the over-sewing completed, remove the tacking and the stiff paper from inside. Then lightly press your work on the wrong side, and pin and tack it in position on the background material. Finish off with small hem-stitches round the edge, and iron on the wrong side again.

Fig. 4 shows a patchwork pattern built up from striped and plain material, using squares and rectangles.

HANDMADE WIRE TOYS

Woman's Own

hese quaint and attractive dolls and animals are made from flexible wire that has been covered with raffia. For the framework it is best to choose bell wire, which is firm and will stay in position when bent.

To make a doll's body, double a length of wire (Fig. 1) and twist together for the neck. Insert another length of wire for the arms (Fig. 2), at right angles to the body. Both arms, outstretched, should be as long as the figure is high, to enable the doll to hold brushes and brooms and other things.

The legs are joined with a curved piece of wire to make the doll stand firmly (Fig. 3).

The framework can now be covered with raffia. Natural-coloured raffia is cheaper than dyed skeins, but not so soft. To make it pliable before using, soak it in water for a few minutes and allow to dry. Coloured raffia does not need soaking as it has already been treated in the dye bath.

Raffia varies in width. Select the wide strands for winding round the body leaving the thin stringy strands for plaits, manes and tassels. Wind raffia firmly round the body, each strand overlapping so that no wire shows anywhere. The legs are covered from the bottom upwards and the arms from the hand

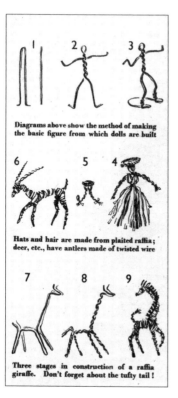

Diagrams above show the method of making the basic figure from which dolls are built

Hats and hair are made from plaited raffia; deer, etc., have antlers made of twisted wire

Three stages in construction of a raffia giraffe. Don't forget about the tufty tail!

to the shoulder so that they do not unravel. Finish off the ends with a darning needle. Do not knot the raffia, as this leaves ugly knobs on the figure. Wind more raffia round those parts of the doll that you want to be thicker.

The clothes are made from strands of coloured raffia all cut the same length. Attach these to the figure and tie at the neck, waist, sleeve, or trouser ends.

Hats are made from thin plaits of raffia sewn into circular shapes (Fig. 4). Hair can be straight or plaited (Fig. 5), or sewn on in raffia loops to look like curls.

TO MAKE THE ANIMALS

(Note that animals such as mountain goats, deer, and other horned creatures such as Fig. 6, need not have their antlers covered!)

To make the frame, start with two pieces of wire the same length. Twist both pieces of wire together, bend into shape for neck and body, and separate for legs (Fig. 7). The frame is then covered in the same way as for dolls (Fig. 8).

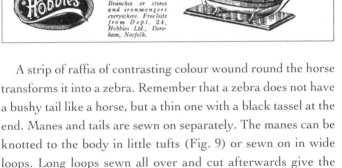
A strip of raffia of contrasting colour wound round the horse transforms it into a zebra. Remember that a zebra does not have a bushy tail like a horse, but a thin one with a black tassel at the end. Manes and tails are sewn on separately. The manes can be knotted to the body in little tufts (Fig. 9) or sewn on in wide loops. Long loops sewn all over and cut afterwards give the effect of shaggy fur if you wish to make llamas, wolves or dogs.

TETHER BALL

Arthur Lawson

This is one of the most surprising games I ever came across. For some reason I could never get interested in Tether Ball for it looked too much like a game designed for three-year-olds. But then one day we made an outfit – and discovered one of the fastest two-handed games we had ever played. But even those first games didn't hold a candle to those that came later when we learned the technique. We found that we had to be on our toes every second of the game, that we had to use skill and speed even against a slow player, but best of all, or maybe worst, we found that everyone wanted to play it at once!

It all sounds too good to be true but I haven't yet exhausted all the virtues of Tether Ball. It is easy to make, remarkably cheap, and takes up very little room. A clear space 20ft square will make the court. A tennis ball, two rackets, a bit of cord and a pole constitute the equipment. What could be more simple?

THE POST

Get a tree, or a pole, about 13ft long and measuring about 3in in diameter at the base. If you are using a tree be careful to pick one that's perfectly straight. Then peel off the bark and paint a black line 2in wide around it 4ft from the top or smaller end. If you are going to make the post from a piece of lumber get some straight-grained wood 3in by 3in and 13ft long. Cut it down with a draw-knife and plane so that it measures 3in square at the base and about 2in square at the top. Then plane down the corners to make it octagonal. Paint the 2in black circle as described above, and the pole is ready.

THE BALL

You can't make the ball but you can buy one. A plain tennis ball is the best. You'll have to make a net for it because it must be tethered to the top of the pole with a piece of cord. Plain chalk-line or heavy fish-line is the best cord to use. You'll need about 10ft of it altogether. Cut the 10ft piece of cord into four even lengths, then look at the diagram [on page 168] and go to it.

Tie two lengths of line together in the middle, using the square knot shown at 'D'. Then tie the other two pieces in the same manner. Now you will have four ends. Tie these together as shown, making a rough square about 1in on the side. Now the job will look like the diagram under '2nd Stage'. Pull all knots tight. If any come loose they were tied improperly. Tie them over again, following 'D'.

Next make four little triangles as shown in '3d Stage'. Tie 1 and 2 together, 3 and 4, 5 and 6, 7 and 8. Now it will look something like '3d Stage'. You have made one square, now, and four triangles. The next thing to do is to make four diamonds. Do this by tying 1 to 4, 3 to 6, 5 to 8, and 7 to 2. The net will begin to look like a basket.

If you have gone so far without mishap the rest is rather easy. Set the ball into the net and tie four more diamonds. Pull them

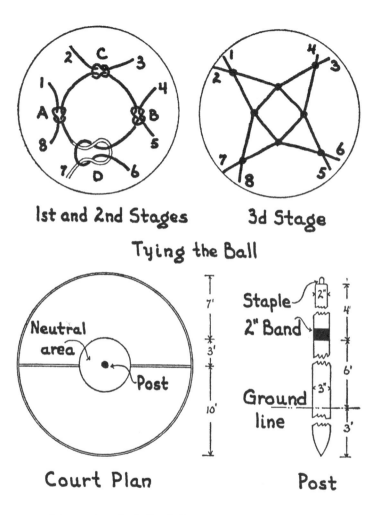

1st and 2nd Stages

3d Stage

Tying the Ball

Court Plan

Neutral area

Post

7'

3'

10'

Post

Staple

2" Band

Ground line

2"

4'

6'

3'

3"

very tight, so that the ball is held securely, and on top of that tie four more diamonds. That will be enough. Divide the eight ends into two parts, four strands in each, and tie a good strong square knot against the ball. Throw in one extra half-hitch for luck and tie the ends together to form a loop. The job is done!

SETTING UP THE GAME

Before putting up the post tie the ball to it. Use high-grade mason's line or very strong fish-line. Chalk-line will not be strong enough and most soft-woven cord will fray quickly. The ideal cord is the so-called cod line. It is tough and strong and light. Tie the cord to a staple or heavy screw-eye on the top of the post. Then 8ft away tie the ball securely to the other end of the cord. When the post is up the ball should hang free 2ft from the ground.

Set the post firmly in the ground. The black circle should be just 6ft from the surface. The post should be secure and solid and should not vibrate when the game is being played. If you bury 3ft of it it should hold anything.

Now mark the court as shown in the diagram. The inner circle is taboo ground. The outer circle is not really necessary but you can put it in if you want to. Be sure to mark the cross line very plainly. In the excitement of the game it's easy for a player to forget where he belongs.

There is only one additional bit of equipment. You'll need two tennis rackets.

THE RULES

The object of the game is to wrap the tether string around the pole above the black line. One player tries to wrap it in one direction and his opponent tries the other direction. The first one to do so wins one point.

1. Players toss for first serve. The winner of the serve has his choice of court; the loser can choose the direction of play.

2. Service is made by the player standing in the center of the court and striking the ball with his racket. He may strike it any way he wishes and in any direction. But if he winds

the string in the opposite direction from the one agreed on at the opening of the game the point goes to the opponent.

3. The receiver must try to keep the server from winding the string around the pole and must try to wind it in his own direction. He may hit the ball any way he wishes, but no player can strike the ball more than once before it has gone into the opposite court.

4. Each player must remain within his own court. This means that he must also keep his arm and racket inside his own court. If he fails to do this, or if he steps into the neutral area it constitutes a foul.

5. A foul is also made whenever the string wraps around a player's racket or arm or other part of his body, or when a player or his racket touches the post.

6. A free hit is allowed the opponent for every foul committed. When a free hit is given the ball must not be intercepted or struck by the player committing the foul until the ball has passed completely through his court once.

7. Game or point is made when the string is wound completely around the pole *above* the black line.

8. After each game or point the service is given to the other player. He can choose the direction in which to wind the ball for that game.

9. A set is won by the player first reaching six games or points with a two game lead.

PARLOUR RACES

Herbert McKay

POTATO RACE

Half a dozen potatoes are placed beside a basin for each competitor. Each is provided with an eggspoon.

At the word 'Go!' competitors have to take up the potatoes, one by one, with the eggspoons and put them in the basin. The potatoes have to be taken up fairly with the spoons. They must not be pressed against the basins, any part of the body, or furniture. They may, however, be pressed against other potatoes.

The first to get the six potatoes into the basin is the winner.

THE ORANGE RACE

This is a team race.

Chairs are placed in two straight lines facing each other, and sufficiently far apart for legs to be spread out on both sides.

Two teams, equal in numbers, sit on the chairs with their legs straight out and their feet on the floor. An orange is placed on the feet of the end player in each team.

171

On the word 'Go!' the players with the oranges transfer them to the feet of the next player on their side. Only the feet may be used in making the transfer. The second player passes the orange on to the third, and so on to the end of the row.

If an orange slips off the feet to the floor, the player who lets it slip must take it back to the leader, who starts it off again. The winning team is, of course, the one which gets the orange to the end player first.

BALANCING RACE

This is one of the most comical of parlour races.

Four or five competitors line up for the race at one end of the room. Each competitor raises a foot and places a small book on it. Books or old magazines of little value should be used for this purpose.

At the word 'Go!' the competitors begin to hop towards the other end of the room, keeping the book balanced on the foot. If it slips off, as very frequently happens, the competitor goes back and starts again.

One length of the room is quite long enough for this race.

THE TORTOISE RACE

Several competitors lie flat on their backs. They then raise themselves on hands and feet without turning over. On the word 'Go!' they race to the other end of the room without turning over.

If any competitor collapses during the race he must remain where he is till he has recovered his position. He must then count ten before starting off again.

HOPPING RACE

Two or more competitors may take part in this race according to the width of the room.

Six or eight nuts are spaced evenly along the room for each competitor, and a small basin is put at the end of each line.

On the word 'Go!' competitors hop to one of the nuts, pick it up, and hop back with it to the basin. When all the nuts are in the basin, the competitor hops back to the starting line. The first to arrive is the winner.

If any competitor lets the raised foot touch the ground, he must put down the nut, if he is carrying one, hop back to the starting line, and start off once more.

THE PEA-AND-STRAW RACE

Twenty dried peas are put in each of four saucers on the floor. About a yard away from each saucer is placed a small basin or another saucer.

Each of four competitors is provided with a straw, the kind used in imbibing liquids. The aim is to take up the peas one by one, by suction through the straws, and to transfer them to the basins.

Competitors start at the word 'Go!' If a pea falls wrongly it must be picked up by suction and without touching it with the hands, before going on to the next pea.

The one to finish first calls out when he has dropped the last pea into the basin, and is declared the winner.

A little laughter adds to the fun of this competition; it serves as a handicap against those given to untimely laughing.

PUTTING THE BABY TO BED

This is a relay race with two teams.

Two large dolls, two cushions, or two bundles are needed; also three lighted candles.

The two teams are lined up. The first in each team takes a 'baby' on one arm and a lighted candle in the hand of the other arm. The Compére holds the third lighted candle.

The Compére gives the word 'Go!'. The two leaders hurry to the other end of the room, round a chair (which must not be touched), and return to the start.

Baby and candle are handed over to Number 2, who does the same, and so on till the whole team has run. The first to finish is, of course, the winning team.

The 'baby' should be sufficiently large to prevent the hand being used to shade the candle. If the candle goes out at any part of the run the competitor must go back and relight it from the Compére's candle; he must then go on and do the run again.

Skill is shown in a nice compromise between speed and precautions against the candle being blown out.

COMFORT FOR CAMPERS

One of the aims of every camper should be *to make himself comfortable*. This calls for a certain amount of improvised equipment in order to keep things clean and dry and to save labour. Improvising equipment is a necessary and enjoyable part of camping and offers scope for skill and ingenuity. All improvised equipment should be strong and serviceable, and dangerous spikes on which campers may get hurt should be avoided, especially at eye level. A few examples of such equipment are described below, but these are only indicative of wider possibilities.

TRIPOD

This has more uses than any other form of improvised equipment. Take three straight pieces of stick, laying these side by side, lash together and then open out into a tripod. This can be used to hold a wash-stand or a rucksack; or four small tripods may support two straight bars between them to make an excellent case-rack.

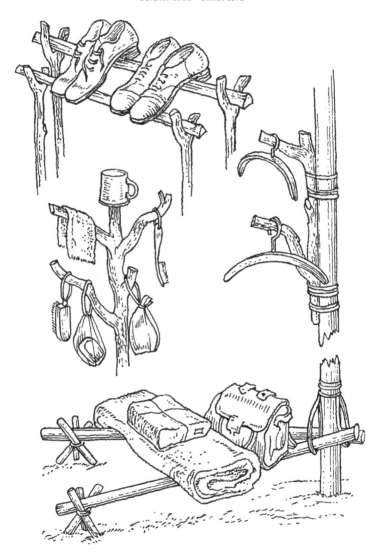

IMPROVISED EQUIPMENT FOR PERSONAL USE

RACK FOR BEDDING, ETC

This is for a bell tent. Fasten two loops to the centre pole about 12in from the ground; slip two stout poles into these, resting the other ends on tripods.

CLOTHES LINE

A good clothes line can be made of two pieces of rope twisted together, the clothes being fastened through the twists.

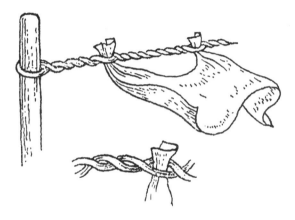

CONVERSION TABLES

All conversions are approximate and have been rounded up or down. Always use one system or the other, do not mix imperial and metric. In 'Clothes and the Home' and 'Fun Things to Make and Do' sections in particular, use the original measurements for the construction items where ever possible, rather than conversions.

OVEN TEMPERATURES

°F	°C	Gas	
225	110	¼	cool
250	130	½	cool
275	140	1	very low
300	150	2	very low
325	170	3	low
350	180	4	moderate
375	190	5	moderately hot
400	200	6	hot
425	220	7	hot
450	230	8	very hot

MAKE THE MOST OF
YOUR MILK WITH
BOURNVILLE COCOA

 1 *Here's the way to make cocoa with a minimum amount of milk.* For each cup you mix a teaspoonful of cocoa and a little boiling water with 1½ teaspoonfuls of sugar into a thick paste. Then fill up with boiling water and finally add two or three teaspoonfuls of cold milk.

Used in this way Bournville Cocoa helps to eke out your limited milk supplies.

 2 TINNED MILK

ONE CUP RECIPE
1 teaspoonful
Bournville Cocoa

1 teaspoonful sugar

2 teaspoonfuls unsweetened concentrated milk

Mix cocoa and sugar to a paste with a little boiling water. Fill up with boiling water and add the concentrated milk.

 3 POWDERED MILK

ONE CUP RECIPE
1 teaspoonful
Bournville Cocoa

1 teaspoonful sugar

2 teaspoonfuls powdered milk

Mix cocoa, sugar and milk powder to a very thick paste with VERY LITTLE warm water and fill up with boiling water, stirring continuously.

And, by the way, it keeps better in a tin

5D
PER ¼ LB

LESS THAN PRE-WAR PRICE

VOLUME

¼ tsp		1.25ml	
½ tsp		2.5ml	
1 level tsp		5ml	
1 level tbsp		15ml	
1 fl oz		30ml	
2 fl oz		50ml	
5 fl oz	¼ pint	150ml	
7 fl oz	⅓ pint	200ml	
10 fl oz	½ pint	300ml	
15 fl oz	¾ pint	425ml	
20 fl oz	1 pint	500ml	
	1¼ pints	700ml	
	1½ pints	850ml	
	1¾ pints	1 litre	
	8 pints (1 gallon)	4.54 litres	1.2 US gallons

WEIGHT

½oz	10g	8oz	225g
¾oz	20g	9oz	250g
1oz	25g	12oz	350g
2oz	50g	1lb	450g
3oz	75g	1½lb	700g
4oz	110g	2lb	900g
5oz	150g	2¼lb	1kg
6oz	175g	3lb	1.35kg
7oz	200g		

MEASUREMENTS

⅛in	3mm	6in	15cm
¼in	5mm	6½in	17cm
½in	1cm	7in	18cm
¾in	2cm	8in	20.5cm
1in	2.5cm	9in	23cm
1¼in	3cm	9½in	24cm
1½in	4cm	10in	25.5cm
2in	5cm	12in (1 ft)	30.5cm
2½in	6cm	3ft (1 yd)	91.5cm
2¾in	7.5cm	1 rod (16.5 ft)	5m
3½in	9cm	10 rods (165 ft)	50m
4in	10cm	1 sq. ft	929 sq. cm
4½in	11.5cm	1 sq. yd	0.83 sq. m
5in	12.5cm		

KNITTING NEEDLES

Old UK	Metric	US
14	2mm	0
12	2.75mm	2
10	3.25mm	3

NOTES

IN THE GARDEN

IN THE KITCHEN

CLOTHES AND THE HOME

FUN THINGS TO MAKE AND DO

SOURCES AND ACKNOWLEDGEMENTS

The compiler and publishers are grateful to those below for permission to include extracts. While every effort has been made to contact copyright holders, in a few cases this has proved impossible. If, in these cases, the copyright holders contact the publisher, we will be pleased to include an acknowledgement in any future editions.

IN THE GARDEN

Material in this section is drawn from booklets published in wartime by the Ministry of Agriculture & Fisheries, in particular *Fruit from the Garden* ('Growmore' Bulletin No. 7), *How to Grow Small Fruits* ('Dig for Victory' Leaflet No. 22) and *Growing Food for Health and Profit: A Guide for all who Dig for Plenty in their Gardens and Allotments* (1947).

A.G.L. Hellyer, 'Storing and Pickling Vegetables' and 'Making the Most of Manures', from *Utility Garden for Home Needs* (W.H. & L. Collingridge Ltd, 1949), by permission of Penelope Hellyer and Octopus Publishing Group.

EATING AND DRINKING

Recipes and information in this section is from the various leaflets produced by the Ministry of Food and HMSO. These include *Preserves from the Garden* ('Growmore' Bulletin No. 3), *Edible and Poisonous Fungi* (Ministry of Agriculture & Fisheries Bulletin No. 23), *How to Grow small Fruits* ('Dig for Victory' Leaflet No. 22), *Fruit from the Garden* ('Growmore' Bulletin No. 7) and *Growing Food for Health and Profit* (HMSO, 1947).

'Catering guide' and 'Tea-time Recipes', from *Good Housekeeping Menus* (compiled by the Good Housekeeping Institute, 1954), by permission of *Good Housekeeping* and the National Magazine Company.

Ambrose Heath, 'From What's Left in the Larder', from *What's Left in the Larder* (Nicholson and Watson, 1940); 'Some Edible Fungi' and 'Fishy Fare', from *Fare Wisely and Well* (Ward Lock, 1951).

Jason Hill, 'Wild Foods for the Table'and 'Some Tasty Tisanes', from *Wild Foods of Britain* (Adam and Charles Black, 1939), by permission of the estate of Dr F.A. Hampton.

E.P. White, 'Wartime Treats', from *Eating with Pleasure: War-time Cookery without Tears* (Rolls House Publishing, London, 1942).

CLOTHES AND THE HOME

This section is drawn from items in the wartime *Make do and Mend* leaflets, articles of the period in publications long defunct, as well as the following sources.

'Plasticine to the Rescue', *Housewife*, May 1951; Lucien Ginnett, 'A Home-made Weather Vane', *Housewife*, May 1951. Philippa Lewis Collection.

Aage Thaarup and Dora Shackell, 'A Cloche and a Fabric Hat', from *How to Make a Hat* (Cassell & Company Ltd, 1957).

'A Jaunty Raglan Jacket' and 'With lace at hand: a Feminine Frill for Gloves', from *Woman Week-end Book* (Odhams, 1950). © IPC+ Syndication.

Joanna Chase, 'When you've been caught in the rain' and 'To Smarten Frayed Wrists', from *Sew and Save* (The Literary Press, Glasgow, 1941). Reprinted by permission of HarperCollins Publishers Ltd © 1941 Joanna Chase.

'Home-made Cleaning Materials', from *The Book of Hints and Wrinkles* (Odhams Press, 1942). © IPC+ Syndication.

'How to Make a Wooden Airer' and 'How to make a Useful Plate Rack', from *Modern Make and Mend* (George Newnes, 1938), by permission of Associated Newspapers Limited.

FUN THINGS TO MAKE AND DO

'Comfort for Campers' is from a Ministry of Eduction leaflet, *Organised Camping* (HMSO, 1948). Other sources for this section are as follows:

Margaret Beresford, 'Puppets Made from Waste Materials', from *How to Make Glove and String Puppets* (Fitzroy Publications, 1948).

'A Tyre Boating Pool', *Housewife*, July 1950. Philippa Lewis Collection.

Lynn Miller, 'The Acrobat' and 'Two Pine-cone Toys to Make', from *How to Make Simple Moving Toys* (Sir Isaac Pitman and Sons, Ltd, 1954).

'A rocking-horse made from coathangers', from *Woman Week-end Book* (Odhams, 1950). © IPC+ Syndication.

L.B. and A.C. Horth (revised by M. Metcalfe), 'An Egg-Cosy' and 'Patchwork', from *101 things for Girls to Do* (B.T. Batsford, 1954), reprinted with permission of Batsford, an imprint of Anova Books.

'For the Top of the Stocking', *Woman's Own*, December 1950. © IPC+ Syndication; Philippa Lewis Collection.

Herbert McKay, 'Parlour Games', from *Party Night* (Oxford University Press, 1940), by permission of Oxford University Press.

Arthur Lawson, 'Tether Ball', from *Homemade Games* (J.B. Lippincott Company, 1934).

The following books have also been useful:

Artemis Cooper, *Writing at the Kitchen Table: Elizabeth David* (Michael Joseph, 1999)

Susan Foreman, *Loaves and Fishes: an illustrated history of the Ministry of Agriculture, Fisheries and Food 1889–1989* (HMSO, 1989)

Jean Grose, *Those Seaside Days: Memories of East Anglian Family Holidays in the 1940s* (Poppyland Publishing, 1986)

David Kynaston, *Austerity Britain 1945–51* (Bloomsbury, 1997)

James Lansdale Hodson, *Thunder in the heavens, being some account of what I have seen and what people have said to me in England and elsewhere between April 3rd 1947 and March 29th 1949* (Wingate, 1950)

Raynes Minns, *Bombers and Mash: The Domestic Front 1939–45* (Virago, 1999)

Sonia Orwell and Ian Angus (eds.), *George Orwell, Collected Essays, Journalism and Letters of George Orwell Vol IV: In Front of Your Nose, 1945–1950* (Secker & Warburg, 1968)

Mollie Panter-Downes, *One Fine Day* (Virago, 1985)

Barbara Pym (eds. Hazel Holt and Hilary Pym), *A Very Private Eye: the diaries, letters and notebooks of Barbara Pym* (Macmillan, 1984)

Michael Sissons and Philip French, *Age of Austerity: 1945–1951* (Penguin, 1964)

The compiler would also like to express her gratitude to the staff of Cirencester and the Bodleian Libraries, and Kate Moore and Emily Holmes at Osprey Publishing.

ILLUSTRATIONS

The publisher is grateful to the following for providing images and permission to reproduce illustrations:

Getty Images: pp.10–11, 85583410; p.70, 102729721; plate section p.7, 90768130

Imperial War Museum: p.23, PST 2893; p.41, PST 59; p.53, D 8336; p.72, D 4273; pp.96–97, D 4857; p.104, V 122; p.114, D 14780; p.123, D 14798; p.139, D 11053; p.159, D 17282; plate section pp.2–3, PST 6079; plate section p.5, PST 14951

Istockphoto.com: front cover and part openers; p.27; p.31; p.38; p.183

Mary Evans Picture Library: p.59 and 181, 10418094; p.63, 10281530; p.130, 10279561

Mirrorpix: plate section p.6, MP65989

Philippa Lewis Collection: p.48; p.76; p77; p.119; p.127; p.133; p.134; p.141; p.146; p.164; p.165; plate section p.1

National Media Museum / Science and Society Picture Library: plate section p.8

V&A Images Victoria and Albert Museum: plate section p.4

Cadbury (Bournville): p.180

Hobbies: p.165

Loft Ladders Ltd: p.133

Courtesy of the McCall Pattern Company: plate section p.1

Premier Foods: p.48, Yorkshire Relish; p.76, Foster Clark Soups; p.77, Oxo

Rentokill Pest Control (British Hermeseal): p.134

Singer (www.singerco.co.uk): p.119

Yeo Paull Ltd (Paull's of Martock): p.178